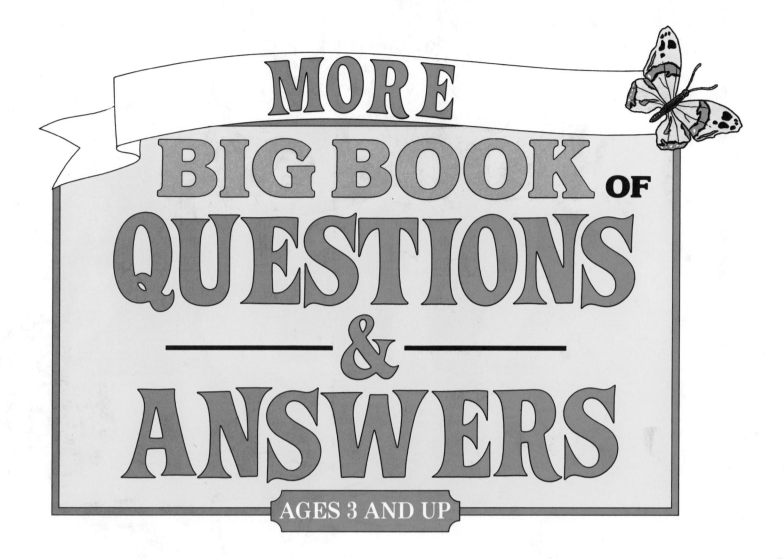

MORE
BIG BOOK OF
QUESTIONS
&
ANSWERS

AGES 3 AND UP

PUBLICATIONS INTERNATIONAL, LTD.

Louis Weber, C.E.O.
Publications International, Ltd.
7373 North Cicero Avenue
Lincolnwood, Illinois 60646

Permission is never granted for
commercial purposes.

Manufactured in U.S.A.

h g f e d c b a

ISBN 1-56173-412-8

Library of Congress Catalog
Card Number 90-61494

Contributing Authors:
Gary W. Davis,
The Learning Source
Teri Crawford Jones

Illustrated by:
T.F. Marsh
Ilene Robinette

CONTENTS

UNDER THE SEA

Q. What does the deepest part of the ocean look like?

A. It would be hard to see anything at the bottom of the sea because there is no light beyond 6,000 feet deep. If you went below with a flashlight, you would see soft mud. You might see thin animal trails in the mud. There are no plants, although some animals like sea cucumbers and sponges look like plants.

Q. What kind of fish do you find deep in the oceans?

A. Strange fish live deep in the ocean. Gulpers look like long tails with huge mouths; oarfish resemble ribbons with horses' heads; and anglerfish and vipers seem like they're from someone's nightmare. Many fish are blind because there is no reason to see in a place so dark. Some fish provide their own light with special organs in their bodies that glow in the dark.

Q. What do fish eat deep in the ocean?

A. Food is scarce at the bottom of the ocean. The fish swim along with their mouths open, eating whatever comes their way. They find parts of animals that died at the surface and drifted down to the bottom. Small fish will eat fish twice their size.

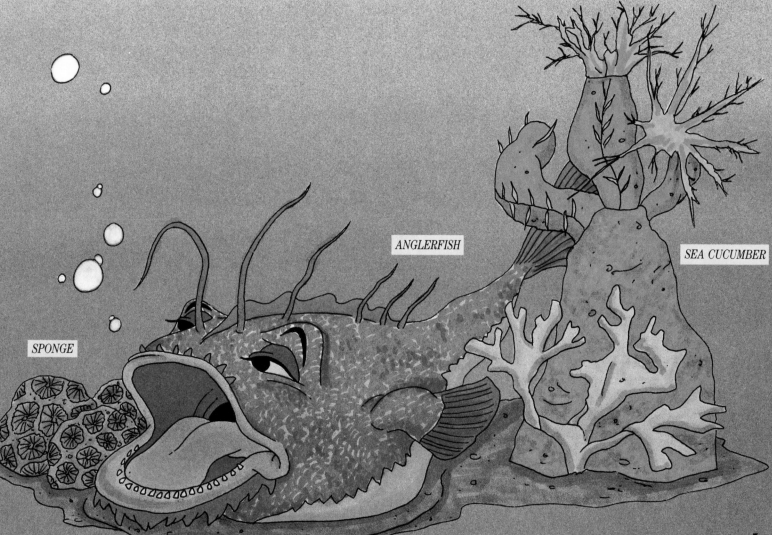

ANGLERFISH

SEA CUCUMBER

SPONGE

Q. Are starfish really stars?

A. No, starfish, or sea stars, are star-shaped animals that live in the shallow part of the sea. They usually have five arms that stretch out from a round body in the middle. However, some kinds of starfish have as many as 50 arms. They use their arms to swim and to look for things to eat on the sea bottom. Starfish come in many different colors—bright pink, red, or dark blue.

Q. What kind of horse is a seahorse?

A. A seahorse is a fish about 12 inches long. Its head looks like a tiny horse's head with its neck proudly arched. It swims standing up with its tail tightly curled. The little fin on its back whirls like a propeller to move it forward. The mother seahorse puts her eggs in the father's stomach pouch. He carries them until they hatch.

Q. Why does the swordfish carry a sword?

A. The upper jaw of a swordfish is very long and pointed. It looks a great deal like a long, thin sword. A swordfish uses this unusual feature to spear its food, such as mackerel, herring, and squid. Swordfish have been known to use their swords on whales and sharks. Sometimes a swordfish will even charge a boat and poke a big hole in the side with its sword.

Q. What kind of fish are stingrays?

A. Stingrays are like underwater birds. These flat fish swim by flapping their winglike sides. Their eyes are on the top and their mouths are under their bodies. Because of the way they are built, stingrays never see their food. Instead, they use touch and smell to find something to eat.

Q. Can stingrays really sting?

A. Stingrays will not sting on purpose. However, if you step on one in the water, it will sting. The sting comes from a sharp spine a stingray has in its tail. When it is startled or threatened, a stingray whips its tail and attacks with its stinger. Rays are hard to see when they rest on the ocean bottom covered with sand, so swimmers have to be careful where they step.

Q. What songs do humpback whales sing?

A. People aren't sure why humpback whales sing, but many songs have been recorded. They moan, burp, thrum, snore, scream, grunt, thump, knock, chirp, whistle, click, and cry in songs that last for up to 30 minutes. During the mating season, they sing beautiful songs.

Q. What kind of animal is an octopus?

A. The shy octopus is a mollusk that lives under rocks or anyplace it can hide. Under each of its eight legs are suction cups for holding onto things. An octopus has no bones, so it can change shape and slide in and out of small spaces. Its mouth is shaped like a parrot's beak, which helps it to tear up food. There are almost 150 kinds of octopuses, from tiny ones to large ones.

Q. How does an octopus protect itself?

A. An octopus has many ways to hide from enemies. It can change color to match whatever it is lying on or swimming through. If it is frightened, an octopus can shoot a stream of black ink. This confuses the enemy while the octopus makes a quick getaway. It can also change its shape from big and round to long and thin. This way it can hide in a hole or a crack in a rock.

Q. What is the difference between an octopus and a squid?

A. A squid and an octopus are close cousins. However, a squid has ten arms while an octopus has eight. Squid arms are usually not as long as octopus arms. Their bodies are also narrower and longer than those of octopuses.

SQUID

OCTOPUS

Q. Why are tropical fish so colorful?

A. Many tropical fish live among pink and red coral reefs. Among these are the bright blue damsel fish or the orange-and-white striped clownfish. Because fish are believed to be color-blind, scientists wonder why tropical fish are so colorful. It seems that color may make no difference. It may be the stripes and shadings of the colors against the coral reef that hide the little fish from their enemies.

Q. What is a coral reef made of?

A. A coral reef is made up of small animals that look a lot like plants. However, corals are related to jellyfish. They grow best in clear, warm ocean water. Corals are like tiny, soft rubber balls that grow together. Around the tops are rings of arms, or tentacles. Their bodies make a mineral-like substance that forms the reefs. When corals die, they become part of the reef.

Q. What kinds of animals live on a coral reef?

A. A coral reef is home to many tropical fish, such as the brilliant blue, red, orange, and yellow angelfish. Green moray eels hide in coral crevices and tiny silvery anchovies dart in and out. Porcupine fish puff out in a spike-covered ball when they spy an enemy. Red and green algae grow on coral.

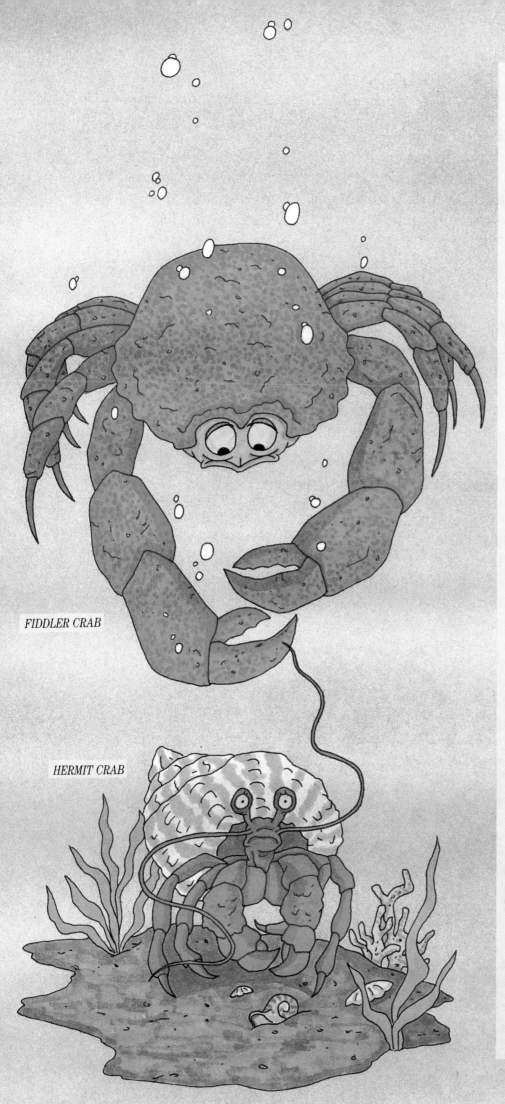

FIDDLER CRAB

HERMIT CRAB

Q. Why does a fiddler crab fiddle?

A. When a male fiddler crab is looking for a wife, it dances. It also looks like it's playing a fiddle, or violin. The fiddle is the largest of its two claws. The bow, or stick it plays with, is the smaller claw. The crab waves its claws up and down, sideways, and around in front of the female. The movement looks like someone is playing a fiddle.

Q. How does a hermit crab protect itself?

A. A hermit crab's rear body is unprotected by the hard shell other crabs have. To solve this problem, the hermit crab backs into someone else's empty shell. It drags the shell behind it like a camp trailer. When a crab grows, it finds a larger home. A hermit crab always takes along little sea anemones on its shell. The anemone's stinging tentacles help protect the crab.

Q. What kind of crab is a horseshoe crab?

A. Even though the horseshoe crab has a hard shell and moves like a crab, it's not a crab. These ancient animals have lived on earth for millions of years. They are different from every other animal. From the bottom, a horseshoe crab looks like a horseshoe with a tail. That's how it got its name.

Q. Where do seashells come from?

A. Seashells are the homes of sea creatures. The shells you find on the beach are empty homes. The owners have died or gone elsewhere. Some shells are made by sea snails. Others are made by soft creatures like clams and oysters. Their bodies make a substance that covers them, then hardens. The hard shell protects them. As they grow larger, some shell creatures move out of one shell and make a bigger one.

Q. What kinds of shells are the prettiest?

A. Everyone has a favorite shell. Many people like the white-and-peach-colored conch shells or the rainbow shine of the clam shell. One of the most beautiful is the nautilus.

Q. How does a pearl get inside an oyster?

A. An oyster's insides are tender and easily irritated. It allows only one kind of tiny shrimp to live inside its shell. However, sometimes other things—such as bits of sand or plants—drift inside. These particles irritate an oyster. An oyster covers these bits with a substance called *nacre* to stop the itching. This substance hardens and becomes a pearl.

DINOSAURS

Q. What does "dinosaur" mean?

A. The name *dinosaur* comes from the Greek language. *Dino* means "terrible" and *saur* means "lizard." The name was invented in 1841 by Richard Owen. He was a scientist who was trying to explain the bones of mysterious ancient animals.

Q. What is a dinosaur?

A. Not all animals that lived during the time of the dinosaurs were dinosaurs. A real dinosaur lived mostly on land. All dinosaurs walked with their legs directly under them like birds, not sprawled to the sides like crocodiles.

Q. How do people name dinosaurs?

A. Sometimes scientists look at the bones of a new dinosaur to see what feature stands out more than others. Then they choose a Latin or Greek word to describe this feature. A dinosaur with a thick nose on its skull might be called *Pachyrhinosaurus* (PAK-ee-rine-o-sawr-us), which is Greek for "thick" (*pachy*) "nosed" (*rhino*) "lizard" (*saurus*). Other dinosaurs may be named for the place where their bones were found or for the person who found the bones.

Q. What did the world look like during the time of the dinosaurs?

A. In the millions of years dinosaurs were on earth, the world changed a great deal. At first, all of the land was one big continent. Then the land began to break up. Mountains rose and seas formed. Swamps became deserts. Finally, flowers appeared everywhere. As the air cooled, forests of big oak trees grew.

Q. Where did dinosaurs live?

A. Dinosaurs lived all over the world. At first, when all of the land was connected into one huge continent, dinosaurs could walk anywhere they wanted to. When the land broke apart, oceans separated different sections. Certain dinosaurs were cut off from other groups.

Q. Were there other animals in the world besides dinosaurs during this time?

A. Even though dinosaurs were the major animals during their time, birds and flying reptiles ruled the skies. Frogs and crocodiles swam in shallow water, while huge marine reptiles prowled the seas. Mammals at this time were tiny mouselike creatures that hid in burrows and trees.

Q. Were there people on earth during the time of the dinosaurs?

A. No proof exists that people were around when dinosaurs roamed the earth. As far as we know, the last dinosaurs disappeared from the earth 65 million years ago. The first known humanlike animals appeared only a few million years ago.

Q. Who was the first modern-day person to find a dinosaur bone?

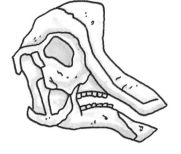

A. People have been finding dinosaur bones for centuries, but they didn't know what the bones were. Some people thought they were human giants. In 1809, someone discovered an *Iguanodon* (ig-WAN-o-don) bone in England. In 1787, someone in Philadelphia found a duckbill thigh bone. In 1802, 12-year-old Pliny Moody found dinosaur tracks in Massachusetts. A dinosaur was finally named in 1824 when William Buckland described his discovery as a *Megalosaurus* (MEG-uh-lo-sawr-us). Early scientists thought all dinosaurs walked on four legs.

Q. How do people put dinosaur skeletons together?

A. The work just begins after dinosaur bones are dug out of the ground. It might take months or years to clean the bones. Then scientists carefully put the bones together in the right order. Large bones have to be hung by ropes. New bones are made from glass fiber to replace those that are missing. The skeleton is arranged in a lifelike pose so that people can see it.

Q. Are there animals alive today that lived during the time of the dinosaurs?

A. You would recognize some of the animals that shared the earth with the dinosaurs in their modern-day cousins. Birds were a part of the dinosaurs' world. There were also lizards, snakes, soft-shell turtles, frogs, salamanders, and an early form of opossum. Some fish of that time look much the same today. And, of course, there were insects.

Q. How are dinosaurs related to birds?

A. Many scientists believe that dinosaurs are the ancestors of birds. Some dinosaurs had feathers, and birds today have reptilelike feet. The skeleton of *Archaeopteryx* (ar-kee-OP-ter-iks) looks a lot like a bird. But it has a long tail and clawed fingers.

Q. What would our world be like if there were dinosaurs today?

A. Our world would probably be much different. From their beginnings, people would have had to compete with dinosaurs for food and try to keep from becoming dinosaur food themselves. It would not have been so easy for people to rule the earth.

Q. What kinds of dinosaurs were there?

A. People who study dinosaurs have so far identified about 340 different kinds. These groups are meat eaters, giant plant eaters, armor-plated dinosaurs, dinosaurs with horns and frills, duckbilled dinosaurs, dinosaurs with thick skulls, and dinosaurs with spikes or plates on their backs.

Q. What were the longest, heaviest, smallest, and fastest dinosaurs?

A. The longest dinosaur may have been the heaviest. Huge *Ultrasaurus* (ul-tra-SAWR-us) bones show a creature over 100 feet long, including neck and tail. It might have weighed from 80 to 150 tons. The smallest adult dinosaur may have been a *Compognathus* (kom-pug-NAH-thus) ("pretty jaw"), which was 1 foot high and 2 feet long. The fastest were the *Ornithomimids* (or-nith-o-MEE-mids) (ostrich dinosaurs).

Q. Were dinosaurs warm- or cold-blooded?

A. Scientists have argued about this question for years. Because dinosaurs were much like reptiles, some say they were *cold-blooded*. This means that outside air warmed them. However, dinosaurs were also a lot like birds, which are *warm-blooded*. This means their blood always stayed the same temperature.

Q. What did flying reptiles eat?

A. Different kinds of *Pterosaurs* (TAIR-uh-sawrs) had a variety of mouth and tooth sizes. This suggests they ate a variety of different foods. *Pteranodons* (tair-AN-uh-dons) had beaks that were a lot like those of today's pelicans. They probably ate fish. Another *Pterosaur* had comblike teeth, which it probably used to gather small creatures and plants from water. Other *Pterosaurs* probably ate insects like modern-day bats do.

Q. Did any dinosaurs live in the ocean?

A. Dinosaurs ruled the land, while the skies and seas were held by reptiles. However, some of the huge reptiles that lived in the ocean looked a lot like dinosaurs. Some were called "ribbon reptiles" because of their long necks. Their feet were like large paddles that pushed them through the water. There were also ocean lizards that grew up to 30 feet long. Other sea reptiles looked something like our modern dolphins, which are mammals.

Q. What did these animals eat?

A. Some skeletons of ocean reptiles survived so well that scientists had an easy job finding out what they ate. A dolphinlike reptile ate fish and flying reptiles. It must have caught flying reptiles by leaping out of the water and grabbing them as they were looking for fish. Other sea reptiles ate fish or hard-shelled clams or mussels.

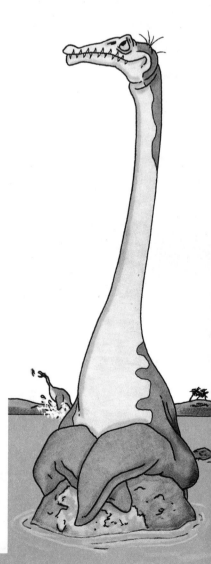

Q. How did the huge *Apatosaurus* (ah-PAT-uh-sawr-us) live?

A. People used to think that the *Apatosaurus* spent all of its time wading in water. New studies show that this huge beast lumbered around on land, staying in big herds for protection, and holding up its long, thick tail to keep it from being trampled on.

Q. How did *Apatosaurus* eat plants?

A. A dinosaur as big as *Apatosaurus* needed a lot of food. A modern 5-ton elephant eats 400 pounds a day. So you can imagine how much a 33-ton *Apatosaurus* ate—at least half a ton! Its teeth, however, were small and not good for chewing. To solve this problem, *Apatosaurus* swallowed stones, which would grind up the plants it ate in its stomach. It used its tremendously long neck to browse through treetops for tasty leaves.

Q. Did *Apatosaurus* lay eggs or have live babies?

A. No one knows for sure, but scientists have reason to believe *Apatosaurus* babies were born live. The largest possible egg would have been 100,000 times smaller than an adult *Apatosaurus*. Tracks left by these dinosaurs show that babies traveled with adults. So they would have had to be large enough and ready to go with the herd as soon after birth as possible.

Q. Why did *Stegosaurus* (STEG-uh-sawr-us) have plates on its back?

A. The first *Stegosaurus* skeleton was found with several triangle-shaped plates near its backbone. But no one knew how to put them on its back or what they were for. Some scientists thought they stuck straight up; others thought they laid flat. Some thought they were for protection; others thought they caught sunlight to keep the dinosaur warm, shedding heat when the dinosaur was hot. The plates may have been decoration.

Q. What was *Stegosaurus* like?

A. This 25-foot, 3-ton dinosaur walked on all fours. Its brain was the size of a golf ball. The end of its tail carried four spikes, which could be used to hit an enemy. It ate only soft plants.

Q. What are duckbilled dinosaurs?

A. The duckbilled dinosaurs all had long heads that ended in front with broad, flat bills. The tops of their heads, however, were quite different. Many duckbills had different sizes of crests made of bone. Others were flat-headed. Duckbills ate plants, twigs, and pine needles. As their teeth wore down, they grew new ones.

Q. How do we know so much about *Maiasaura* (mah-ee-uh-SAWR-uh)?

A. In 1978, dinosaur hunter Jack Horner was looking for small dinosaurs in Montana. The tiny bones someone else had found turned out to be baby dinosaurs. Horner dug in the same place and found a dinosaur nest with fossilized eggs and little dinosaurs. Most of them were *Maiasaura*. Nearby he found the bones of young and adult *Maiasaura*.

Q. What does *Maiasaura* mean?

A. *Maiasaura* means "good mother lizard." The discovery of a *Maiasaura* nest with eggs and the bones of young dinosaurs showed that a mother dinosaur must have been around to care for them. The babies' teeth showed that they had been eating tough plants, which the mother would have brought to the nest.

Q. What was life like for a *Maiasaura*?

A. Bones found in Canada show that *Maiasaura* moved long distances during the year to find food. From the remains of nests in Montana, scientists know that *Maiasaura* traveled to special places to lay their eggs and raise their young.

Q. Why do people think *Tyrannosaurus Rex* (tie-RAN-uh-sawr-us reks) **was the fiercest dinosaur?**

A. *Tyrannosaurus* means "tyrant lizard." A tyrant is someone who is a cruel ruler. This huge meat eater was well named. It stood over 18 feet high and weighed over 5 tons. Its 3-foot long jaws held 60 very sharp teeth. It ran after large horned dinosaurs and duckbills on powerful back legs that had 8-inch claws on the toes.

Q. What did *Tyrannosaurus Rex* **use its two tiny front arms for?**

A. *Tyrannosaurus Rex* had very tiny arms compared to the rest of its body. Each of these arms had two fingers ending in long claws. These arms must have been used for something, but scientists are not sure for what. Some think they may have been used to help *Tyrannosaurs* stand up after resting so they wouldn't fall forward on their faces. These arms may also have been used to hold their dinner.

Q. Were there other dinosaurs like *Tyrannosaurus Rex?*

A. There were many other meat-eating dinosaurs that looked like *Tyrannosaurus,* although they weren't as big. Their smaller size meant they were faster runners than *Tyrannosaurus.* Their front legs, or arms, were larger than the ones *Tyrannosaurus* had.

Q. What did dinosaurs eat?

A. Dinosaurs ate a wide variety of things. Some dinosaurs ate nothing but plants. They munched on leaves, ferns, flowers, and water plants. The large meat eaters ate other dinosaurs. Smaller meat-eating dinosaurs lived on bird and dinosaur eggs and hunted mammals, reptiles, and small dinosaurs.

Q. What kind of families did dinosaurs have?

A. At first, people thought each dinosaur roamed around by itself. But new discoveries of bones and nests show that many kinds of dinosaurs lived in herds like antelopes and elephants do today. The males may have fought each other for females. Most females probably laid eggs and sat on them or covered them with sand or plants to keep them warm. They brought food to their babies.

Q. How did dinosaurs get their food?

A. The smaller plant-eating dinosaurs probably ate plants and fruit close to the ground. The small two-footed dinosaurs were fast runners. They could chase other small animals, leap into the air for insects, or use their hands to pick up eggs. Large and fast meat eaters may have attacked plant eaters or eaten already dead animals. The largest plant eaters with long necks could reach into treetops or under the water for plants.

TRICERATOPS

STYRACOSAURUS

Q. What did armored dinosaurs look like?

A. Armored dinosaurs were about the size of tanks. They had tough leathery skin with thick plates of bone covering their backs, heads, necks, and tails. Even their eyelids had plates. Short spikes of bone stuck out from their sides. Their long tails ended in a hard club, which sometimes had spikes. Their legs were short and wide.

Q. How did _Triceratops_ (try-SAIR-uh-tops) live?

A. _Triceratops_ ("three-horned face") was the largest horned dinosaur. It stood almost 10 feet tall and weighed about 6 tons. Behind its head was a broad shield that stretched over its shoulders. Its three horns were about 40 inches long, which is as long as a broom handle. Herds of _Triceratops_ roamed the plains eating plants. It probably had few enemies.

Q. What did other horned dinosaurs look like?

A. Many of the other horned dinosaurs looked a lot like _Triceratops_ although they were smaller. Some had very long shields behind their necks. Others had only one horn sprouting from the nose, or a bony plate on its nose in place of a horn. The _Styracosaurus_ (sty-RACK-uh-sawr-us) had six long spikes along the edge of its shield.

ANKYLOSAURUS

BIRDS

Q. How are baby birds fed?

A. When mom or dad bird returns to the nest with food, the babies will either peck at the parent's bill or open their mouths wide so that their parents can drop in something tasty. The parents must work very hard—their babies are growing fast and are always hungry.

Q. How do bird parents protect their babies?

A. If an enemy approaches their babies, some birds fly at it, beating their wings and screeching. Other birds flutter on the ground like they have an injured wing, so that the enemy will follow them rather than look for the babies. Storks keep their babies from getting sunburned by shielding them with their wings. Penguin parents put all of their babies in the middle of an adult circle to shelter them from cold winds.

Q. How do baby birds learn to fly?

A. Somehow even when they are little, birds know what to do to fly. Young eagles practice flapping their wings for hours to gain strength. Most of the time, when their feathers have grown strong enough, birds just leap into the air. They may be awkward getting up to that first leap, but once they are in the air, they do everything just right.

Q. Why do birds sometimes shed their feathers?

A. Bird feathers wear out and get dirty just like your clothes do. Sometimes, they even break. So at least once a year, a bird drops its old feathers and grows new ones in a process called *molting*. Birds usually molt a few feathers at a time so that they can still fly while they grow new ones. Ducks and geese, however, cannot fly while they are molting. But they still can swim.

Q. Why do birds have so many different kinds of feet?

A. Birds' feet depend on where they live. Tree-dwelling birds have three clawed toes in front and one in the back to help them perch on branches. Woodpeckers have two toes in front and two in back for walking up tree trunks. Swimming birds have webbed feet. Those that walk on soft ground have wide feet to keep them from sinking. And meat-eating birds have talons that can grasp and hold small animals.

Q. Why do birds have so many different kinds of beaks?

A. Since birds have no teeth, they need beaks specially suited for catching and eating food they like. Hooked beaks are good for tearing meat or fruit and cracking nuts. Long, sharp beaks can spear fish or pick bugs from holes. Beaks in the shape of scoops are good for filtering water to find tasty bits to eat. And flat beaks can be used to pry open clams.

Q. Are eagles really bald?

A. Bald eagles are not bald—they do have feathers on their heads. People may have called them bald when they first saw them from a distance because their white head feathers against the dark brown body feathers made them look bald. Bald eagles' heads are not white until they are 5 or 6 years old. Up to that time, they are a splotchy brown and white all over.

Q. How can hummingbirds stay in one place in the air?

A. Anyone who watches a hummingbird at a feeder marvels at how the tiny bird can stop in mid-air to eat. Its wings move so fast that people see nothing but a blur. Hummingbirds' wings are different from those of other birds—they are stiff and move like a wrist and elbow. A hummingbird moves them forward and back, twisting them at the same time. This movement keeps the bird up, but stops it from going forward.

Q. How can hummingbirds eat with such long, thin beaks?

A. Hummingbirds drink flower *nectar,* which is a sweet liquid found in the middle of flowers. To get to the nectar, the hummingbird needs a long, thin beak that can reach deep into the flower. When people feed hummingbirds, they put up a feeder with a long, thin tube filled with sugar water. They color the water red to attract the birds, just like they are attracted to the color of their favorite flowers.

Q. Are owls really wise birds?

A. The owl has become a symbol of wisdom because it looks wise. An owl's big, wide-open eyes make it look like it knows a lot. But "the wise old owl" really has a small brain for a bird of its size. If you say someone is as wise as an owl, you are really calling him or her a birdbrain.

Q. Why do owls have such big eyes?

A. Owls have big eyes because they are evening and night hunters. They need to be able to see small things move in the dark from far away. The barn owl can find a mouse in light 100 times dimmer than the light people need to see. Owls also have excellent hearing. If they can't spy a mouse right away, they will be able to hear where it is.

Q. What is a kiwi?

A. Kiwis are little birds that live in New Zealand. They have such small wings that they cannot fly. Their thin, coarse feathers look more like hair than feathers. In fact, a kiwi's pear shape, lack of tail, and unusual feathers make it look a little like a hairy football on short legs. Kiwis come out only at night to hunt for worms, insects, and berries.

Q. Why do some birds disappear during the winter?

A. Watch the birds around you. You may see some birds year-round, while others are only around in the spring and summer. The birds that seemingly disappear have *migrated*. This means they have flown to a warmer place, usually south, where there is food to get them through the winter. They leave in the fall and return in the spring.

Q. Where do birds go when they migrate?

A. Some birds only go a short distance. Others travel the world over. The Arctic tern migrates from the top of the world to the bottom. It travels up to 25,000 miles. Some birds go from North to South America; others go from Europe to Africa.

Q. How do migrating birds know the way to faraway places?

A. Birds' amazing ability to travel thousands of miles and know how to get there and back home has always been a mystery to scientists. They have found that birds use a wide variety of cues to keep them flying in the right direction. Some birds may use mountains, rivers, and coastlines. Others may use the sun's position and star patterns. Some even hear the right way to go.

Q. How does the oxpecker help other animals?

A. If you went to Africa to see antelopes, giraffes, rhinos, and hippos, you are also likely to see oxpeckers. These birds spend most of their day walking all over these huge animals looking for ticks, flies, and other bugs. Big animals allow these birds to hang around, because they want to get rid of these buggy pests.

Q. How do pelicans catch fish?

A. Pelicans have a great big pouch attached to their lower beak. This pouch can hold three gallons of water. Brown pelicans fly over the ocean looking for fish. When they see one, they dive into the water. When they come up, they have a pouch full of water and fish. As they fly away, they dip their pouches a little to let the water drain out. A pelican can eat 20 pounds of fish a day.

Q. How do wild birds help people?

A. Wild birds make people's lives better in many ways. Many birds eat thousands of insects that might otherwise eat the food we grow or hurt our trees. Other birds help to control the number of rats and mice, thereby reducing the damage caused by these animals. Some birds eat dangerous snakes. In some parts of the world, people hunt birds for food. Many people just enjoy watching beautiful birds.

Q. How did roadrunners get their name?

A. When people see roadrunners, these desert birds are usually racing alongside a road. Roadrunners are not good flyers because of their short wings, but their long legs make them good runners. Roadrunners can dash up to 15 miles an hour to catch their food, which may be a mouse, a snake, a lizard, or a spider.

Q. How do roadrunners live in the desert?

A. Roadrunners are well suited to life in the hot desert. They eat many different things, getting enough liquid from fruit, seeds, and eggs without having to look for water at all. They also have thick feathers to protect them from rattlesnake bites. Roadrunners' nests are made of things the birds find in the desert, such as sticks, snakeskins, and dried animal droppings.

Q. Why do woodpeckers peck on trees?

A. Woodpeckers use their heads and tough, straight beaks to drill holes in tree bark just like you pound a nail into wood with a hammer. They do this to find little bugs that live under the tree bark and in the tree trunk. When they find a bug, they use their long tongues to pull the tasty treat out of the tree.

Q. Does pecking hurt trees?

A. You might wonder whether all the pounding and drilling woodpeckers do is bad for trees. Actually, woodpeckers are really helping trees. They eat bugs and pests that burrow into wood and would finally kill a tree if it weren't for the woodpecker's help.

ANIMALS

Q. Are koala bears really bears?

A. Koala bears look a little like teddy bears with their round ears and round, furry bodies. However, they are really *marsupials,* just like kangaroos. This means they carry their babies in a pouch. They live in Australia along with most of the world's other marsupials.

Q. What are koalas like?

A. Koalas have very soft fur. They like humans and will cuddle up to you if you hold one. They are also very smart. They spend most of their time in trees, coming down only at night to find food. They are heavy and a little clumsy, so they move rather slowly.

Q. Why are koalas not good pets to have?

A. Koalas are not easy to take care of. They eat one unusual thing—eucalyptus leaves. They even get most of their water from these leaves. Eucalyptus trees are not common everywhere and are not the easiest plants to grow. If you don't have eucalyptus trees, a koala cannot survive. Surprisingly, any other animal that tried to eat these leaves would be poisoned.

41

Q. Are bats blind?

A. Bats are not blind. Their big eyes are made for seeing in the dark. Bright sunlight actually hurts their eyes. Bats can quickly catch little insects that people can't even see. They also use their ears to find insects. When bats squeak, this sound hits something—such as an insect—and bounces back. A bat's big ears pick up the sound, telling it where the insect is.

Q. How do bats sleep?

A. Bats sleep during the day in caves, hollow trees, or cracks in rocks. Their favorite place is a cave. Thousands of bats sleep hanging upside down. Their back feet have strong claws that they use to hang onto the ceiling. Bats sleep close together and wrap their wings around their bodies to keep themselves warm.

Q. How do bats help people?

A. Bats eat thousands of pesky insects such as mosquitoes. They also spread flower and tree seeds. Without bats' help, certain flowers and fruit trees would not be able to live. There would also be a lot more insects to bother people.

Q. Do porcupines really "shoot" their quills?

A. Those who have been unlucky enough to get too close to a porcupine may believe that a porcupine shot its quills at them. But a porcupine can't do this. When it becomes frightened, as it easily does, its quills stand straight up. A porcupine then turns its back on its enemies. The long quills in its back come loose easily and stick in whatever brushes against them—a person's hand, a dog's face, etc.

Q. Why are porcupine quills so hard to get out of things?

A. Once a porcupine quill has stuck to something, it is very difficult to pull out. This is because the quills are covered with very small barbs that point backwards. When a person or animal who has been stuck tries to shake them out, the quills just stick more. Grabbing a quill and pulling is the only way to get it out.

Q. Why does a porcupine need sharp quills?

A. A porcupine is slow moving and clumsy. Many animals might think it would be a tasty treat. So it uses its quills to protect itself. The quills also help a porcupine to swim. The hollow quills are full of air, which keeps the porcupine afloat as it paddles along.

AYE-AYE

AARDVARK

DUCKBILLED PLATYPUS

Q. Is a duckbilled platypus a mammal, a reptile, or a bird?

A. A platypus is a little like all of them. This animal has fur and feeds its babies milk like a mammal, lays eggs like a reptile, has a beak that looks like a duck's, and a tail like a beaver's. Scientists believe the platypus is both a reptile and a mammal.

Q. What is an aardvark besides the first word in the dictionary?

A. An aardvark looks somewhat like a pig with a long snout and donkey ears. However, it is no relation to a pig, nor to any other living animal. It is in a family by itself. They have sharp claws and sticky tongues for breaking into termites' nests and eating them.

Q. What kind of animal is an aye-aye?

A. An aye-aye is a lemur, which is a monkeylike creature. It lives in Madagascar, an island off the eastern coast of Africa. The aye-aye has long fingers and clawlike nails.

Q. Is a manatee a real animal?

A. Yes, you can find manatees in tropical rivers. They are often called sea cows, probably because they are so large. Manatees can grow to 15 feet and weigh nearly a ton.

MANATEE

Q. Why does a chameleon change color?

A. A chameleon is a lizard that lives in trees. Its skin color usually blends with its environment. Temperature, sunlight, and emotion affect this animal in an unusual way. A chameleon can go from black to brown to green to bright red and yellow. An excited or frightened chameleon turns paler; an angry one turns darker. Hot sunlight can cause it to turn almost black, while darkness causes it to lighten.

Q. How does a chameleon change colors?

A. A chameleon has special cells under its skin that have different colors in them. These colors are called *pigments*. A chameleon's pigment cells can become bigger or smaller and change its color. You have pigment in your skin, too. It makes you the color you are.

Q. What else can a chameleon do?

A. A chameleon is a strange animal in many ways. Each of its pop eyes can move by itself to look in all directions. It has a long, curly tail just like a monkey's that can hold onto branches. It also has a long, sticky tongue that quickly snaps out to catch flies. It has three horns—one on its nose and two on his head. These make a chameleon look almost like a dragon.

Q. How do penguins live in such cold places?

A. Penguins have bodies that are built for the coldest weather on earth. Their oily feathers are close together, which keeps out the cold wind and keeps in their body heat. They have a thick layer of fat all over their bodies to keep them warm. In cold water, their bodies heat up just enough to keep them comfortable.

Q. What do penguins find to eat in all that ice and snow?

A. Penguins get all of their food from the ocean. They are very good swimmers and divers. They catch fish, crab, and squid. They also eat small sea creatures called *plankton*. Penguins often eat snow when they are thirsty. They can also drink salty ocean water without getting sick.

Q. Why do penguins have wings if they can't fly?

A. Penguins' wings are really more like flippers. These flippers are perfect for "flying" underwater. Penguins use their strong wings and webbed feet to pull themselves along as they hunt for fish. When they are ready to get out of the water, they swim very fast toward the shore. Then they leap out of the water and land on their feet on the ice.

Q. Are Santa's reindeer real animals?

A. Real reindeer can be found across the northern part of North America, Europe, and Asia. In North America, they are called *caribou.* Across the northern part of Norway, Sweden, and Finland, people called *Lapps* herd reindeer like cattle. They use reindeer for food and clothes, and to pull their sleds and carry loads. People even make knives from a reindeer's huge antlers.

Q. What is a moose like?

A. A moose is a large deer that looks very clumsy. It has a huge head with an overhanging lip that looks a little like a trunk. It has long legs and huge horns. Its wide feet help it to walk on soft, muddy ground. Even though they are large and powerful, moose are gentle animals.

Q. What does a moose eat?

A. A moose loves to eat leaves and little twigs. In the summer, it will wade into lakes to eat water lilies. Sometimes, it dips its head underwater to eat, then comes up wearing a hat of water lilies on its big horns. A moose's favorite food is mushrooms. If it sees people picking mushrooms, it will raid their baskets.

Q. Do hippos spend all of their time in the water?

A. The only time hippos come out of the water is to eat grass at night when the air is cooler. Even though hippos have thick skin, they sunburn easily. Hippos are also easily scared. They feel safer at night. During the day, they swim or sleep in the water.

Q. How big are hippos?

A. A full-grown hippo weighs almost 4 tons. That's 8,000 pounds! A male hippo can be 14 feet long. You would need to stand on the shoulders of two adults who are standing on each other's shoulders to be as tall as a hippo is long. A newborn hippo weighs only 100 pounds. It gains about 10 pounds a day. While small, the baby rides on its mother's back in the water.

Q. Why do hippos need such big teeth if all they eat is grass and other plants?

A. A hippo's white, sparkling teeth are larger than any other land animal's teeth. They use their teeth mostly to chew leaves and grass. Sometimes, males fight with their teeth. But the main reason hippos need big teeth is to defend themselves against crocodiles. They live everywhere hippos do, and they eat meat. A full-grown hippo is too big for a crocodile to attack. But baby hippos are in danger when crocodiles are around. Mother hippos fiercely protect their babies.

Q. How do elephants talk to each other?

A. Many people may have heard an elephant's loud trumpeting. But that's only one sound elephants use to talk to other elephants. They also roar, growl, and rumble. Many rumbles are so low people can't hear them. These low rumbles can travel a long way.

Q. How are African elephants different from Indian elephants?

A. African elephants naturally live in Africa, while Indian, or Asian elephants, live in southern Asia. African elephants are larger than their Indian cousins. They have very large ears, which they use like fans to cool themselves. African elephants have two "fingers" at the end of their trunks, while Asian elephants have only one.

Q. How do elephants take care of their babies?

A. Female elephants travel together in family groups. They all help take care of and protect the babies. They show them good plants to eat and how to dig for water. If a little elephant screams, all the big elephants rush to see what is wrong and to help the baby out of trouble.

INDIAN ELEPHANT

AFRICAN ELEPHANT

Q. Why are chimpanzees a part of circuses?

A. Chimpanzees are thought to be the smartest apes. When they are young, chimpanzees are easy to train. They like to copy what people do, so it takes them only a few days to learn tricks. They also make many different sounds, hand movements, and facial expressions that look a lot like what people do. People enjoy watching these personable apes make monkeys out of people.

Q. Why are monkeys usually so noisy?

A. Monkeys like to talk to each other. They talk about food, danger, and play. They often gather in one tree to talk to each other. Sometimes, they become angry if someone tries to take their space or their food. Instead of fighting, many monkeys will screech and howl at each other. This saves anyone from getting hurt, even though the noise can be hard on the ears.

Q. What is the smallest and the largest ape and monkey?

A. Apes are the largest *primates*, which is what all monkeys and apes are called. The largest ape is the gorilla. A gorilla can stand over 6 feet tall and weigh 500 pounds. The smallest monkey is a tiny, fuzzy animal called the *pygmy marmoset*. It is about 6 inches tall and weighs about 3 ounces.

Q. Is a white rhino really white?

A. The white rhino is actually a grayish color. It is called "white" because someone did not clearly hear it described as "wide." And a wide animal it is. It grows up to 15 feet long, stands over 6 feet high at the shoulder, and may weigh 7,000 pounds. There is also a black rhinoceros, but it is only a little darker gray than the white rhino.

Q. Why do rhinos charge moving things?

A. Rhinos have very poor eyesight, but they have very good hearing. When they hear something moving, they run toward it just to see what it is or to run over it if they think they are in danger. White rhinos do not charge often. However, black rhinos will often charge at a great speed for no visible reason.

Q. What is a rhino's horn made of?

A. African rhinos have two horns. The larger one is on the nose; the smaller one is right behind it. These horns feel as hard as bone. But they are really made of tightly packed hair fibers. The horns grow constantly. The front horn may reach a length of 5 feet.

Q. What is snakeskin like?

A. Many people believe snakes are wet and slimy because they often appear shiny. However, a snake's skin is dry to the touch. Snakeskin is made up of many smooth, small scales. Snakes come in many colors and patterns including brilliant red, black, yellow, and coral.

Q. Why do snakes shed their skin?

A. Snakes need new skin several times a year. They may be growing or their old skin may become worn and dried out. Since they can't change their clothes like you do, they get rid of the old skin in a process called *molting*. Snakes rub their noses against a rough surface until the skin breaks. They move around while their bodies slide out of the old skin.

Q. Where do poisonous snakes live?

A. Some poisonous snakes, such as rattlers and copperheads, live in the United States. However, the poisonous snakes that cause people the most trouble live in India, southeast Asia, and Africa. These are the cobra, the boomslang, and the mamba. The taipan in Australia is also a snake to avoid. If you want to live in a place with no snakes at all, go to the Arctic, Ireland, New Zealand, or the Azores.

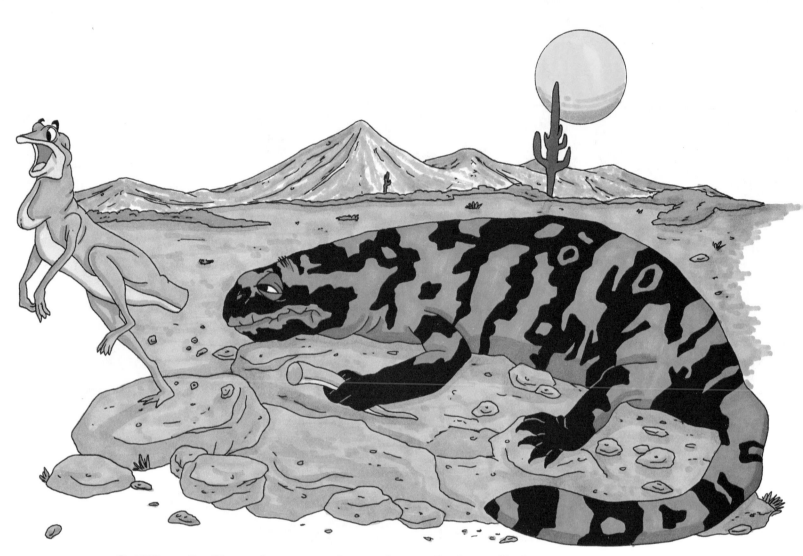

Q. Why do lizards sometimes lose their tails?

A. The tail is the longest part of a lizard. When people or other creatures try to catch a lizard, they naturally grab onto their tails. The lizard, of course, gets scared and wants to get away. The muscles at the base of its tail pinch the skin and bone. Suddenly, the tail comes off and the lizard runs away. After a few weeks, a lizard grows a new tail.

Q. Is the gila monster really a monster?

A. The gila (HEE-LA) monster is a big desert lizard. People may have called it a monster because it can grow up to 2 feet long. It also has powerful jaws that carry a poisonous bite. When it's angry, a gila monster hisses loudly. Its body is covered with tiny, black and pink bumps, which look like little beads. A gila monster can go without eating for several months, living off the fat in its big tail.

Q. Were there ever real dragons?

A. Long ago, people believed huge, scaly dragons flew through the air and burned villages with fiery breath. No one today believes in dragons. But in Asia and Africa you can find monitor lizards that grow 10 and 12 feet long. The rare Komodo dragon is a 9-foot lizard with a big, ruffled fin along its back.

Q. How are turtles and tortoises different?

A. Turtles and tortoises all belong to the same family. Tortoises live in dry places. Turtles are more often found near and in water, along the edges of and in ponds, rivers, lakes, and ocean coasts. Tortoises have square stumpy legs for walking on land. Turtles have flippers for swimming. Tortoise shells have a high dome, while turtle shells are flatter.

Q. How big can turtles get?

A. Certain types of land turtles and sea turtles weigh many hundreds of pounds. The giant turtle is so large a child can ride on its shell while it walks along. The largest turtles and tortoises usually live on islands. They may become giants because there are no animals large enough to attack them or to compete with them for food.

Q. How long can turtles live?

A. Turtles live for a very long time. A box turtle can live over a hundred years. One turtle that died by accident in 1918 was 152 years old. Imagine how long it might have lived if there had been no accident! Some people say that turtles might be able to live for many hundreds of years. No one has been able to prove this because turtles outlive the record keepers.

TORTOISE

TURTLE

Q. How do cats purr?

A. Some scientists think that happy cats purr—such as when they are curled in your lap. Their throat muscles relax and their vocal chords loosen. Breathing causes the chords to vibrate, making the purring sound. Other scientists say they have heard angry and frightened cats purr. They say the purr is not just in the throat. Only a cat really knows how it purrs.

Q. Why do cats rub against your legs?

A. Cats rub against you, the furniture, and anything else to mark everything as theirs. Cats have small oil glands behind their ears and along their lips. By rubbing against things, they leave a scent that only other cats can smell. Your cat is telling other cats that "this furniture and this person belong to me."

Q. Why do hamsters run around on wheels?

A. Hamsters are very active when they are awake. They love to jump on things, go down burrows, swing, and run around. The little exercise wheels that come in hamster cages are especially fun. They will go round and round for an hour or more. Hamsters become bored easily. A bored hamster droops and has dull eyes and fur.

Q. Do goats eat anything and everything?

A. Goats eating tin cans is a well-known picture. However, goats can't eat cans. They are really after the tasty glue under the labels. In fact, goats are picky eaters. They won't eat garbage or food thrown on the ground. They like fruits and vegetables. Goats *can* eat many things that other animals can't, such as sharp brambles and briars.

Q. Why do many farmers keep goats?

A. Farmers have kept goats in many parts of the world for thousands of years. Goats give people milk to drink and for making cheese. Goatskin is made into gloves, jackets, shoes, and boots. Some people think goat meat is better than lamb or beef. Angora goats have silky thick hair, which is used to make sweaters and coats. Some farmers just like goats because they are smart and easy to care for.

Q. How do mountain sheep climb steep cliffs?

A. Mountain sheep have special hooves. Each hoof has two toes. The bottom of each toe looks like a black rubber cup with a hard rim. These toes can hold onto any rock surface. Mountain sheep have strong legs that help them jump onto narrow ledges and sharp rocks. They also have a good sense of balance so they can leap from rock to rock as easily as you run down a sidewalk.

PEAS

Q. What sizes do horses come in?

A. The biggest horses are called *draft horses*. They were used for big farm jobs, such as pulling plows and freight wagons. The largest draft horse is the Shire. It stands almost 6 feet tall at the shoulders and weighs over 2 tons. The smallest horses are ponies. The Shetland pony stands only 39 inches high.

Q. Are there any wild horses in the world today?

A. There are still some mustangs left in the American West. These horses are not true wild horses because their ancestors were tame horses that escaped from people. In Asia and Africa, true wild horses are reddish-brown Przewalski horses and black-and-white striped zebras.

Q. What kind of horses did knights in shining armor ride?

A. Some movies you see show knights in armor riding on regular-sized horses. Just think how heavy that metal armor must have been. In the days of knights, horses wore armor, too. A regular horse could not carry all that weight. Knights had to have big, strong horses. They used big draft horses like Belgians and Shires. These horses were tall and muscular. Carrying a knight in full armor was an easy job for them.

Q. What kind of animals are hyenas?

A. Hyenas look a little like big dogs. They have short, bushy tails and powerful necks and jaws. Their shoulders stand higher than their back legs. They live in Africa and Asia. Most people think hyenas are *scavengers,* which means they eat the meat that other animal hunters leave behind. However, hyenas do hunt on their own. What they catch is often stolen by lions, who are too lazy to go get their own food.

Q. Why do people call hyenas "laughing hyenas"?

A. You may have seen cartoon hyenas laughing wildly. Hyenas do not really laugh like people do. However, they do make a call that sounds a little like wild human laughter. They also make a variety of snarls, howls, grunts, and barks.

Q. Why are badgers always so busy?

A. Badgers are some of the world's best diggers and they spend a lot of their time doing just that. They can dig themselves underground in only a few minutes. They dig to find food and to make a burrow for sleeping or as shelter from bad weather. Badgers are very picky about their burrows. In the summer, they often dig a new burrow every day.

WOLF

Q. Why are people afraid of wolves?

A. Many old stories are about wolves that chase and attack people. In the old days, wolves meant danger. They carried off farmers' calves and lambs; they were thought to be cruel and evil. Wolves are not like this at all. They attack people only if they fear for their lives. They are meat eaters and hunt other animals, just like people do.

Q. Why do wolves howl?

A. Wolves howl to talk to other wolves. Their howls let other wolves know they are around and where their territory is. Wolves may also howl to stay in touch with members of their family. Some people who study wolves say they have seen wolves howl just for the fun of making noise together.

Q. How smart are coyotes?

A. Coyotes are some of the smartest animals around. Many ranchers do not like coyotes because they believe these animals kill calves and lambs. But no matter what traps they set, coyotes quickly figure them out. Coyotes always keep a sharp lookout for people. If they see someone, they quietly trot away. Their gray and tan fur blends in with the bushes and the ground.

COYOTE

INSECTS & CREEPY CRAWLERS

Q. What are insects?

A. Insects are animals that do not have bones inside of their bodies like people do. Instead, they have a hard covering around the outside. Their bodies are divided into three parts. They have three pairs of legs and one set of feelers. Most of them have wings. Common insects are flies, bees, crickets, and ants.

Q. How does an insect grow?

A. An insect egg hatches as a *caterpillar,* or *larva,* which is a small insect without wings. As a young insect grows bigger, its hard outer covering does not grow with it. Instead, a new skin grows under the old one. The old skin splits open, exposing the new one. This process is called *molting.* Caterpillars grow up to be butterflies and moths. Young insects are grown when they develop wings.

Q. How do crickets chirp?

A. Crickets have two pairs of wings. At the base of the front set of wings, there is a special spot that makes a chirping sound when the wings are rubbed together. Only male crickets chirp.

Q. Do cricket chirps tell the temperature?

A. A cricket's body temperature changes with the temperature around it. When it is hot, a cricket chirps rapidly. When it is cool, a cricket chirps slowly. You cannot, however, tell what the exact temperature is by counting a cricket's chirps.

BUTTERFLY

CATERPILLAR

ANT

Q. Why do mosquito bites itch?

A. Only female mosquitoes bite. When they do, they make little holes in your skin with sharp parts of their noses. As they take a little blood, some of the liquid, or *saliva,* from their mouths enters into your skin. This saliva irritates the skin and causes it to swell and itch.

Q. Why do mosquitoes bother some people and not others?

A. Some people are just tastier to mosquitoes. People's natural skin oils vary, so some might smell and taste better to insects. Mosquitoes may also be attracted by perfume or something nice smelling a person has put on his or her skin. Some people also believe that mosquitoes are fonder of people with lighter skin.

Q. Why do fleas live on animals?

A. Fleas are flat, tiny insects that live by biting animals or people and taking a little of their blood. After eating, a flea does not stay on an animal. It will jump off to take a rest nearby. When it is hungry again, it waits for the animal to come back and jumps on it again. When you see a dog or cat scratching or suddenly biting itself, it is probably trying to stop a flea from biting.

MOSQUITO (ENLARGED)

FLEA (ENLARGED)

67

Q. Why do people say "ugh" when they see a slug?

A. Slugs are not pretty creatures. They look like snails without shells and are soft and slippery. Some slugs even bite. As they crawl slowly over plants and rocks, they leave a slimy trail behind them. This slime is a slug's protection. It tastes so terrible that its enemies usually leave it alone. However, fireflies don't care. They like slugs for dinner anyway.

Q. Do all spiders spin webs?

A. Not all spiders spin webs to catch their food. Trap-door spiders live in burrows that they close with a lid made of silk. When they sense movement outside, they open the door, rush out, and grab their dinner. Desert tarantulas leave their homes under rocks at night to hunt for insects and lizards to eat. The bola spider spins a line that it throws over a moth's wings.

Q. What kind of dragon is a dragonfly?

A. When people first saw these little insects, they may have thought they looked like tiny dragons with big tails. Dragonflies have long, thin bodies and legs and big wings and heads. Dragonflies use their legs for catching insects in the air instead of for walking. They live in marshes near rivers and ponds.

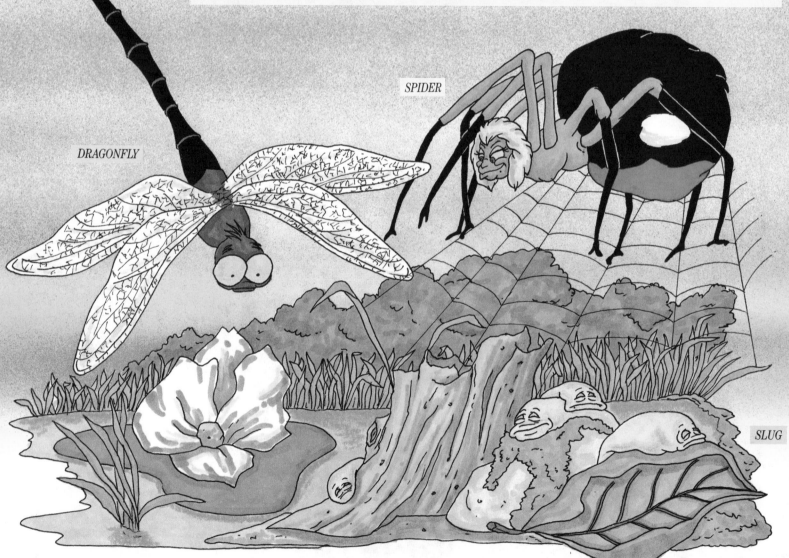

DRAGONFLY

SPIDER

SLUG

Q. Do moths eat clothes?

A. You, or someone you know, may have had a wool sweater or scarf that ended up with a "moth" hole in it. However, the flying moth was not the one who made the hole. A very tiny moth that you may not notice at all often lays its eggs in wool. The small *larvae*, or wormlike creatures that hatch, are the ones that eat the wool.

Q. How are moths and butterflies different?

A. Moths and butterflies belong to the same insect family and are often hard to tell apart, even though there are differences between them. Most moths fly at night, while most butterflies prefer daytime. Moths are usually not as brightly colored as butterflies. When a moth is resting, it folds its wings flat. A butterfly holds its wings up or spreads them out.

Q. Why do people get upset about termites?

A. Termites bother people the world over because they eat wood. Their favorite place is in damp wood where they dig long tunnels and big rooms for their colony to live in. These tunnels weaken the wood, causing it to eventually collapse. If termites live in your house, you may find holes in wood and collapsed floorboards. And because books and some furniture are also made from wood, these insects often eat these items, too.

Q. Why do fireflies light up?

A. Fireflies blink and flash at dusk in the summertime. They are sending signals to other fireflies in the hopes of finding a mate. Fireflies recognize each other by the length and color of the flashes. There are over 2,000 different kinds of fireflies in the world.

Q. What does a praying mantis do?

A. The "praying" part of a mantis's name comes from the two slender "arms" near the front of the insect's body that look like praying hands. A mantis hunts by standing as still as a statue for hours. Its green body blends perfectly with the green leaves, while its huge eyes watch for any movement. When another insect flies by, the mantis jumps forward and grabs it with its spine-covered arms. A mantis then swiftly eats its dinner.

Q. What is a walkingstick?

A. If you see a twig suddenly walk down a tree branch, don't think that you're imagining things. What you're really seeing is an insect known as a walkingstick. The shape and color of its body look so much like a real wooden twig that you can't see it when it stands still. This disguise protects the insect from its enemies. Some walkingsticks even have wings that look like leaves when they're spread out.

Q. Why do snails move so slowly?

A. Snails only have one big foot. Muscles in their foot move it backward. When a snail wants to move forward, it uses wavelike motion. This takes time. They also wait until the slippery substance that comes from the glands below their skin smoothes their path. This substance makes the going easier for tender-footed snails.

Q. Why do people dislike cockroaches?

A. To most people, cockroaches mean dirt. They love to walk in garbage and other dirty places. Then, they move into people's homes, leaving germs wherever they go. Cockroaches are hard to see because they run when you turn on the light. They are also hard to swat because they move so fast. And they are hard to kill because a few roaches always survive the bug spray. Cockroaches multiply quickly and can take over your kitchen very fast.

Q. Why are cockroaches so amazing?

A. Cockroaches are among the toughest animals on earth. They can eat almost anything and survive for weeks with almost no food. They can live almost everywhere, no matter if it's too hot or too cold for everything else. Even radiation won't kill a cockroach! Cockroaches have been around since the time of the dinosaurs.

Q. How do honeybees know where to find flowers?

A. Some bees in a hive fly away to look for flowers. When they find some, they return and tell the other bees by doing a dance in which they wiggle their bodies, flutter their wings, and move in a figure 8 or other form, depending on the distance. Bees gather round and watch. The dance tells the other bees in what direction and how far away the flowers are.

Q. What is a queen bee?

A. A queen bee is the largest bee in the hive. She lays thousands of eggs that grow up to be worker bees. She is well cared for by the workers. If something happens to a queen bee, a hive is not likely to survive.

Q. How do bees make honey?

A. Bees gather a sweet liquid called *nectar* from flowers. They bring this nectar back to the hive in their stomachs where it is put in an empty, six-sided cell made of beeswax. While the nectar is in the bees' stomachs, chemicals are added to it. While the nectar sits in the cell, the water in it dries up and the chemicals turn it into honey.

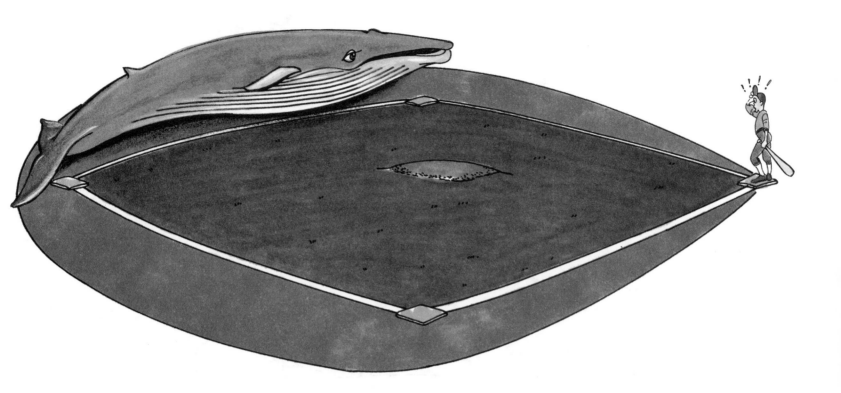

Q. What is the biggest animal?

A. The biggest animal in the world is the blue, or sulfur-bottom, whale. It grows to a length of up to 100 feet. That makes this giant of the seas as long as the distance between the bases of a baseball diamond. Blue whales can weigh up to 300,000 pounds, or as much as 80 good-sized cars.

Q. What is the biggest snake in the world?

A. The longest snake ever found was 37½ feet long. It was an anaconda and lived in South America. The longest snake ever kept in a zoo was a python named Colossus. It was 29 feet long and weighed 320 pounds.

Q. What animal has the biggest ears?

A. The elephant does. Its ears can grow to almost 4 feet in length. Horses and ostriches, by the way, have the largest eyes of any land creature. Their eyes are about 1½ times as big as those of an adult person.

Q. What is the world's smallest bird?

A. The smallest bird is the bee hummingbird. It is only 2 inches long—the size of a piece of macaroni! This amazing bird flies straight up and down like a helicopter when it wants to get nectar from flowers.

Q. What is the world's fastest creature?

A. The world's fastest creature is a bird called the duck hawk. It flies through the air at almost 180 miles an hour. The cheetah, a large cat from the plains of Africa, is the fastest animal on land. It can reach speeds of 70 miles an hour. There are fish that can swim almost as fast. A sailfish, for example, has been clocked swimming in the water at almost 65 miles per hour.

Q. What animal lives the longest?

A. Box turtles, which can be found in backyards in many parts of North America, often live to be over 100 years old. In fact, some have lived as long as 123 years.

Q. What bird flies the farthest?

A. In the autumn, many birds fly off to a warmer place for the winter. They return in the spring when the weather is better. Each year at the end of August, the Artic tern leaves the islands of the Arctic Ocean and flies south to Antarctica near the South Pole. The following June, it flies all the way back to the icy waters of the North Pole. The trip is 11,000 miles each way.

ALASKA

RHODE ISLAND

Q. What is the largest state in the United States?

A. The largest state is Alaska. It has 591,004 square miles. The smallest state is Rhode Island, with only 1,212 square miles. Alaska is more than 500 times bigger than Rhode Island.

Q. What is the country's largest national park?

A. Yellowstone National Park, founded in 1872, is both the largest and the oldest national park in the United States. It spreads over three states—Wyoming, Montana, and Idaho.

Q. What is the tallest building in the United States?

A. The tallest building is the Sears Tower in Chicago, Illinois. It is 1,454 feet high. But that's not the country's largest building. That record belongs to the Boeing 747 Manufacturing Plant in Everett, Washington. That factory covers almost 47 acres.

Q. What is the longest bridge in the country?

A. The longest span belongs to the Verrazano Narrows Bridge in New York, which reaches 4,360 feet. The highest bridge is the Royal Gorge Bridge of Colorado. It is 1,053 feet above the water.

Q. What is the world's smallest country?

A. The answer is Vatican City—the home of popes and the center of the Roman Catholic Church. Even though it is only 0.17 of a square mile in size, it is considered a separate country.

Q. What is the world's largest country?

A. The largest country in size is the Soviet Union, or the Union of Soviet Socialist Republics. It has more than 8 million square miles. The second-largest country, Canada, has a little under 4 million square miles. So the largest country in the world is more than twice as large as the second-largest country in the world.

Q. What country in the world has the most people?

A. China has more people than any other country with just under 1 billion 77 million. Every fifth person in the world lives in China. It is also the third-largest country in size. China is so crowded that almost 300 people live on each square mile of land. There are only eight people per square mile in Canada.

Q. What's the lowest temperature ever recorded?

A. On July 21, 1983, it went down to 128°F below zero at the Soviet Antarctica station of Vostok. That was quite a bit colder than the coldest temperature ever recorded in America. That record-breaker was 80°F below zero at Prospect Creek, Alaska, on January 23, 1971.

Q. What are the world's largest trees?

A. The world's largest trees are the giant sequoias of California. Their usual height is about 275 feet, which means they are about as tall as a 27-story building.

Q. What's the highest temperature ever recorded?

A. On September 13, 1922, it reached 136°F in Azizia, Tripoli, in North Africa. It was almost as hot in Death Valley, California, on July 10, 1913. It reached 134°F on that day.

Q. What is the rainiest place in the world?

A. About 460 inches of rain fall on Mount Waialeale, Hawaii, making it the rainiest place in the world.

Q. What was the worst storm in history?

A. It's hard to determine what the worst storm was. The storm that claimed the most people—300,000 lives—was a cyclone in Bangladesh, near India. This was in 1970.

Q. What was the worst earthquake in history?

A. In 1976, an earthquake in Tangshan, China, killed 750,000 people. This was the worst earthquake in modern history.

Q. What is the brightest star in the sky?

A. Scientists divide stars into six types based on their *magnitudes*, or brightness. Stars of the first magnitude are the brightest. Stars of the sixth magnitude are the faintest, or least bright. Of all the stars in the sky, Sirius is the brightest.

Q. Who was the first person to fly across the United States in an airplane?

A. The first person to cross the country in an airplane was Calbraith P. Rodgers, who did it in 1911. He flew from Sheepshead Bay, New York, to Long Beach, California. The trip took him 49 days. What took him so long? The plane crashed more than 15 times during the trip. By the time it landed, almost every part in the plane had been replaced at least once.

Q. Who was the first person to fly faster than sound?

A. Charles ("Chuck") Yeager was the first person to travel faster than sound, or to "break the sound barrier." He did this in 1947, flying in a Bell X-I rocket plane.

Q. What is the fastest plane around today?

A. The fastest passenger plane is the SST—the supersonic transport plane called the Concorde. It holds 100 passengers and flies through the air at over 1,500 miles an hour. It can make the trip from New York City to Paris, France, in about 4 hours.

Q. What's the fastest car in the world?

A. The world's fastest cars aren't really cars. They're rockets, and they look more like missiles than automobiles. The fastest of these rocket cars belongs to Hal Needham. Stan Barrett drove this vehicle—called *Budweiser Rocket*—at Edwards Air Force Base, California, on December 17, 1979. It attained a speed of 739.666 miles per hour, making it the only land vehicle to break the sound barrier.

Q. What was the most popular movie ever?

A. There are many ways to judge how popular a movie is. Among these are how much money a movie made, how much a movie influenced moviemaking, how many people bought or rented a movie, and others. If you look at how much money they made, the biggest movie of all time was *Batman.* The second-place film was *E.T.* and the third—*Star Wars.* Of course, another movie may come out and set a new all-time record.

Q. What was the most popular TV show?

A. More people watched the last episode of the TV series *M*A*S*H* than any other show. On February 28, 1983, more than 50 million people tuned in to say good-bye to one of their favorite shows.

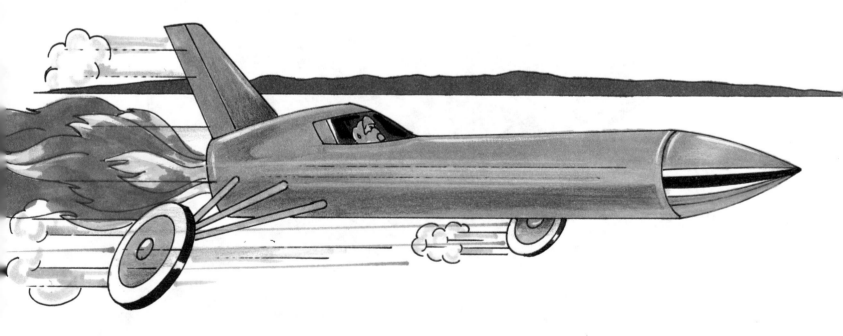

Q. Who has the most hits in the game of baseball?

A. The professional baseball player who had the most hits in a career was Pete Rose. His career lasted 24 years—mostly with the Cincinnati Reds. He had 4,256 hits. That's 65 hits more than the second-place finisher, the great Ty Cobb.

Q. Who stole the most bases?

A. That record belongs to Lou Brock of the St. Louis Cardinals. He stole 938 bases during his career, 46 more than Ty Cobb.

Q. What pitcher won the most games in baseball?

A. The pitcher with the most wins is Cy Young, who won 511 games. He won more than 20 games each year for 25 years. The pitcher who won the most games in a single season was Jack Chesboro. He won 41 games back in 1904.

Q. Which team has won the most World Championships?

A. The New York Yankees have won 22 championships during their history. The second-place winners are the St. Louis Cardinals with nine.

Pete Rose
4,256

Ty Cobb
4,191

Q. Who scored the most points in professional basketball?

A. In a game against the New York Knicks in 1962, Wilt Chamberlain scored 100 points. As a career scorer, Kareem Abdul-Jabbar is the winner. He scored a total of 37,639 points while playing for the Milwaukee Bucks and the Los Angeles Lakers.

Q. Which football player ran the farthest in one year?

A. Eric Dickerson of the Los Angeles Rams ran for 2,105 yards in 1984. He outran O.J. Simpson, who held the earlier record of 2,003 yards.

Q. Which player scored the most touchdowns in a season?

A. The record belongs to John Riggins of the Washington Redskins. He scored 24 touchdowns in 1984. The most touchdowns scored by a player in one game is six. Ernie Nevers set the record in 1929. Dub Jones tied the record in 1951, as did Gale Sayers in 1965. So far, no professional player has managed to score seven times in one game.

Q. What was the tallest wig in history?

A. This question might seem silly at first. But the answer will surprise you. During the 1700s, women in England and France wore wigs that were sometimes up to 4 feet high. They powdered the wigs with flour and covered them with stuffed birds, plates of fruit, and even models of ships.

Q. Who was the oldest person to ever live?

A. A Japanese man from Asan, Tokunoshima Island, Japan lived until he was 120 years and 237 days old. Shigechiyo Izuma was born on the island on June 29, 1865 and died at 12:15 P.M. on February 21, 1986, after developing pneumonia. He was the oldest person whose age was kept record of.

Q. What was the largest unit of money ever made in the United States?

A. At one time, the United States Treasury printed a $100,000 bill. It bore the head of Salmon Portland Chase (1808–73), who was the Secretary of the Treasury during the Civil War. None have been printed since July, 1955. Only 348 of these bills remain in circulation.

Q. Who was the tallest person who ever lived?

A. Robert Wadlow, who was born in Illinois in 1918, grew to be 8 feet 11 inches tall. He weighed 491 pounds. That's about as tall as a child standing on an adult's shoulders! Wadlow was 6 feet tall by the time he was 8 years old. At 15 years old, he was 7½ feet tall.

Q. In which country do people eat the most?

A. According to most experts, Americans eat the most. On the average, each American eats 286 eggs, 80 pounds of fruit, 100 pounds of vegetables, 117 pounds of potatoes, and 116 pounds of beef each year.

Q. Who was the hungriest person who ever lived?

A. There were two very hungry people in history. Back in the 1800s, a woman in London, England, used to eat three loaves of bread, three pounds of steak, a pound of cereal, lots of vegetables, and at least 20 glasses of water every day. In Philadelphia, a boy once ate nonstop for 15 hours each day for a whole year. The whole time he kept saying he was hungry.

Q. What food is eaten the most in the world?

A. Rice is the main food of over half the people in the world. More than 15,000 different kinds of rice are grown the world over.

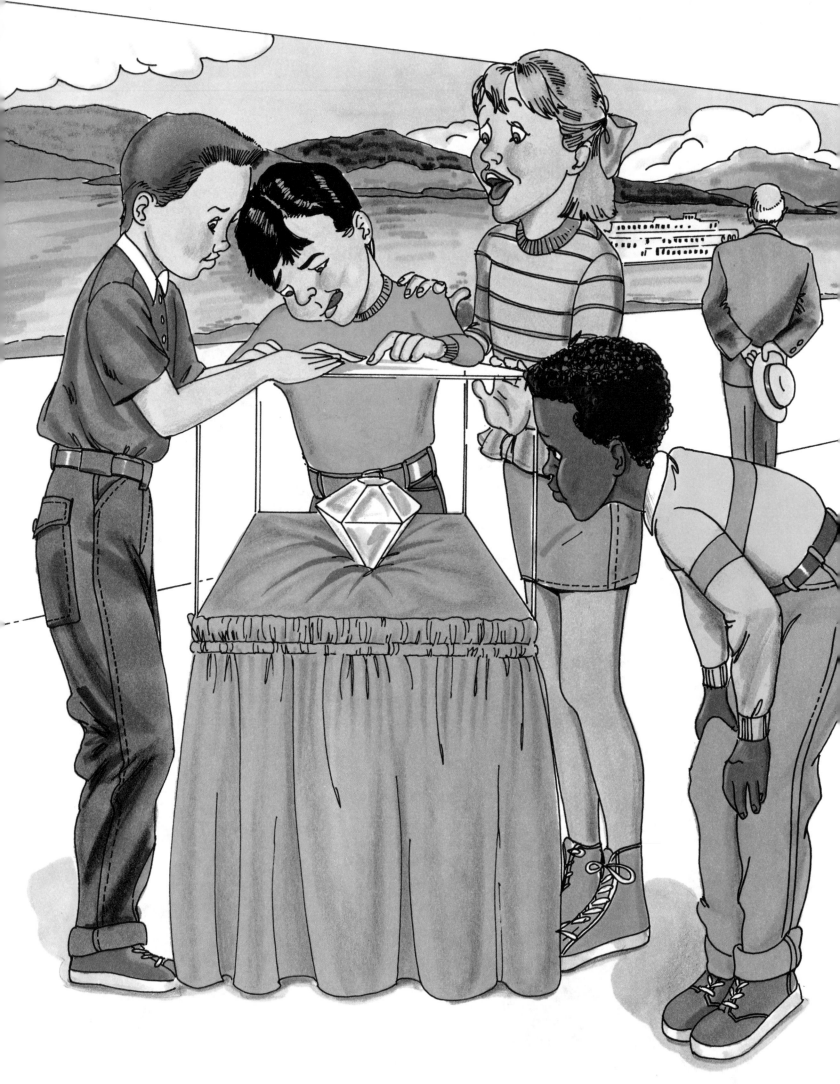

Q. What is the highest number in math?

A. There is none. All you have to do is add the number 1 to any number and you've got a higher number. The highest number that scientists have a name for is the *centillion*. It's a 1 followed by 600 zeros.

Q. What was the biggest diamond ever found?

A. The largest diamond ever found measured 3,106 carats before it was cut. It weighed over 20 ounces. The stone was found by Sir Thomas Cullinan, who brought it to England from South Africa in 1905. The diamond was cut into several stones, including the famous "Star of Africa." The largest diamond ever found in the United States was 40 carats. It was discovered in Arkansas.

Q. What is the longest painting ever made?

A. In 1846, an American artist named John Banvard painted a picture that was 3 miles long and 12 feet wide. It showed the Mississippi River—the biggest river in the United States.

Q. What is the longest place name in the world?

A. A small town in Wales is called Llanfairpwllgwyngyllgogerychwyrndrobwllllantysiliogogogoch. It is usually called Llanfair P.G. for short.

Q. Do the people of Africa all speak the same language?

A. Many languages are spoken in Africa. In fact, more than 700 different languages are used in southern Africa alone. One of the most wonderful African languages is called *Khoisan*. It is sometimes called "the click language" because many words are spoken by making clicking sounds with the tongue or throat.

Q. What kinds of clothes are worn in Africa?

A. In the southern part of Africa, people often wear clothes with bright colors. Many people also wear colorful necklaces, bracelets, and earrings. In the western part of Africa, men often wear long robes.

Q. Are there shopping malls in Africa?

A. Many parts of Africa are as modern as the United States. There are shops, department stores, and even shopping malls. But many parts of Africa are like they were hundreds of years ago. People shop in open-air markets. Farmers, merchants, and others bring what they want to sell to the market each day. Goods are set out on tables or in boxes. Shoppers walk through the rows of wares. When they see something they want, they just stop and buy it. Then they go on to another area, or *stall,* to look for other items they need.

Q. Do Arabs always wear turbans?

A. For thousands of years, the people of the Middle East have wrapped cloth around their heads. It protects them from the wind and the hot desert sun. It is usually called a *keffiyeh*.

Q. Who are the Arab people?

A. Arab people live all over the world. Many live in northern Africa and the Middle East. In fact, there are almost 185 million Arabs living in this area. Many of them follow the religion of Islam, which was founded about 1,300 years ago by Mohammed.

Q. Do Arabs really ride camels?

A. Northern Africa and the Middle East are quickly becoming as modern and up-to-date as any other place in the world. However, it is still possible to see people traveling on "the ships of the desert," as camels are sometimes called. Camels have been used in the desert for ages. They are strong, so they can carry either people or heavy loads. And, even more importantly, they are able to walk a long distance without stopping for water. This makes camels just about perfect for traveling around in the desert.

Q. What is a *kibbutz*?

A. A *kibbutz* is a special kind of farm in Israel. All of the farmers share property and they all work together like a family. Everyone eats together in a big dining hall. The children all live together in a separate home. Parents join their children after work, for religious occasions, and for special holidays.

Q. What is a *sabra*?

A. Over the years, Jews born in Israel were called *sabras*. Where does the name come from? A *sabra* is a fruit, very much like a cactus, that grows in Israel. It is tough and prickly on the outside, but sweet on the inside. Jews born in Israel took the name of this fruit as their own nickname. They felt it described them very well—tough enough to live in Israel, but tender inside.

Q. Do only Jews live in Israel?

A. Most of the people in Israel are Jews. The country was started in 1948 as a safe homeland for the Jews of the world. But almost 15 percent of the people living in Israel are Arabs. The constitution of Israel guarantees people of other religions the freedom to practice their own religion.

Q. What do children in China do for fun?

A. Like everywhere else in the world, Chinese children love sports. Baseball, softball, basketball, ping pong, soccer, and volleyball all are popular.

Q. Was spaghetti really invented in China?

A. Yes, and Chinese cooks still use noodles in dozens of different ways. The compass, gunpowder, paper, porcelain, and silk cloth were also first invented in China.

Q. Why are bicycles so important in China?

A. China is a crowded country. It is also a country in which not many automobiles are made. This makes bikes a perfect way to get around. In fact, millions of people use bicycles to go to work, to shop, or to go to the movies.

Q. What is a Mao jacket?

A. In China, most people dress for comfort instead of style. One of the most popular pieces of clothing in China is a loose-fitting jacket that was made famous by the Chinese leader, Mao Zedong. People around the world started calling these jackets, which are worn by millions of Chinese men and women, Mao jackets.

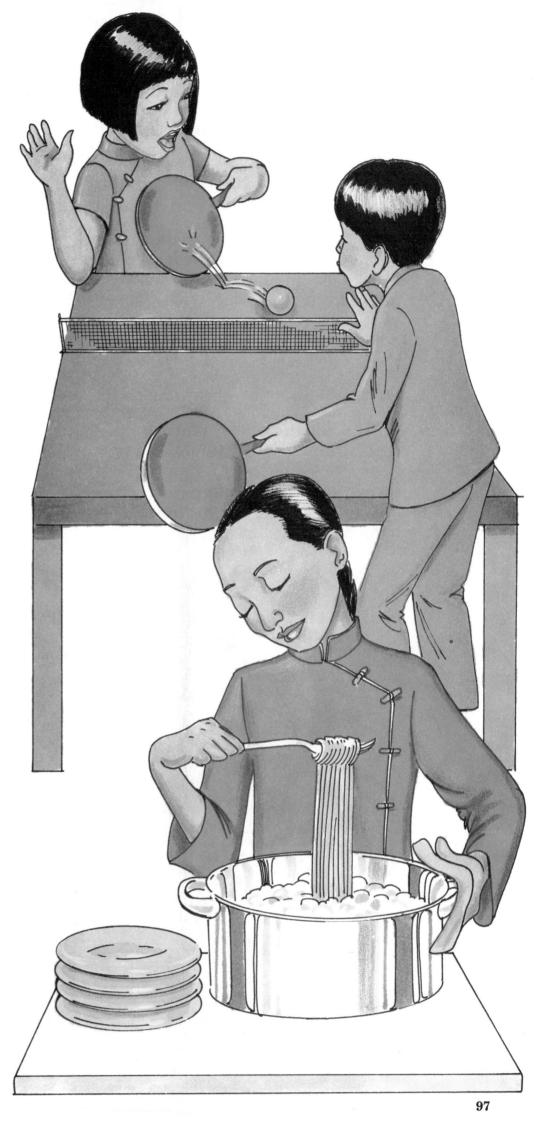

Q. Do people in Japan really eat raw fish?

A. Raw fish—or *sushi*—is popular in Japan and in many other places, including the United States. The people in Japan also eat dishes like *sukiyaki,* which is beef cooked with noodles and vegetables, and *tempura,* which is fried fish and vegetables.

Q. Do Japanese people always wear robes?

A. Today, many people in Japan dress just as we do. But robes, or *kimonos* as they are called, are the traditional way of dressing. Men, women, and children all wear them. A *kimono* is tied around the waist with a sash called an *obi.* Today, *kimonos* are worn mostly on special days—holidays, weddings, and other occasions.

Q. What sports are popular in Japan?

A. The Japanese are great baseball fans. They also enjoy a special kind of wrestling called *sumo. Sumo* wrestlers are big and heavy. Some of them weigh up to 400 pounds. When they get into a ring, they try to bump each other out. The Japanese also love fencing. One of the favorite kinds is *kendo,* in which people use bamboo or wooden sticks.

Q. Did hot dogs really start in Germany?

A. Frankfurters and sauerkraut both came to the United States from Germany. Germany actually has dozens of different kinds of hot dogs, which are called *Wurst.*

Q. How did the Volkswagen get its name?

A. In the 1930s, people in Germany wanted to build a car that everyone could afford. They wanted it to be inexpensive to buy. They also wanted it to last a long time and be easy to fix. Since it was intended to be a car for everyone, they decided to call it the "people's car." And that's what it was called: the *Volks* (the German word for "people") plus *Wagen* (the German word for "car").

Q. What are those short pants that people in Germany wear?

A. *Lederhosen*—leather shorts—have been worn in some parts of Germany for hundreds of years. Today, people wear them mostly for fun, on holidays, and on other special days. The outfit is usually made up of leather shorts with broad leather suspenders. Often, a man or boy also puts on knee socks and a green hat.

Q. Are French fries really French?

A. Those skinny fried potatoes we all love so much were invented in France. Today, however, they are eaten all over the world. In fact, many people, including the French, believe that the best French fries are actually made in France's neighboring country, Belgium. In Belgium as well as in France, those potatoes are simply called *pommes frites*—fried potatoes.

Q. What is the *Tour de France?*

A. The *Tour de France* is the biggest sports event in France. It's like the World Series and the Super Bowl all rolled up in one. The *Tour de France* is a bicycle race. More than a hundred professional bike racers take part. The race lasts over a month, and the cyclists race around the country, doing many miles each day. Fans think it is the hardest, most difficult sports event in the world.

Q. What is the Eiffel Tower?

A. The Eiffel Tower is one of the great landmarks of Paris, France. It looks like a giant iron skeleton rising up over the city. The Eiffel Tower was built for the Paris World's Fair in 1889, and it stands almost 1,000 feet tall.

Q. Do people in England speak the same language we do?

A. The people of England speak English, but many words we use are quite different. In America, for example, we have "trucks." In England, they drive "lorries." Americans ride up and down in "elevators." In England, people use "lifts." American cars run on "gasoline." In England, they use "petrol." An American listens to a "radio." An English person turns on the "wireless." There are hundreds of other words that we do not have in common.

Q. Who goes to public school in England?

A. In England, "public schools" are actually private. They are hard to get into and parents pay a fee to send their children there. Most English children go to regular schools, just as children do in America.

Q. Do people in England really have tea parties?

A. Tea time has been an important part of life in England for hundreds of years. Tea and a small snack are served around 4 o'clock in the afternoon. Usually, this snack is a cracker, a cookie, or a small sandwich. Today, people are so busy that they sometimes don't have time for tea. But many people in England still enjoy the old-fashioned habit of stopping everything for a cup of hot tea.

Q. Do men in Scotland really wear skirts?

A. For hundreds of years, men in Scotland have worn *kilts*. These are skirts that come down to their knees. They are usually plaid. Although years ago they were worn every day, today they are worn only for special holidays and celebrations.

Q. Are there leprechauns in Ireland?

A. Over the years, Ireland has been famous for many things. One of these is the leprechaun, a tiny elf who is supposed to live in Ireland. Although there are thousands of stories about these little creatures, no one has ever been able to prove that they exist—or do not exist.

Q. What is the Irish Derby?

A. The Irish Derby is probably the biggest sports event in Ireland. It is a horse race that the whole country wants to know about.

Q. Who was Saint Patrick?

A. Saint Patrick is honored throughout Ireland. He was born in Britain around the year 400 A.D. and was taken to Ireland as a slave when he was a child. Later in life, he became a priest and returned to Ireland to bring the Christian religion to the country. He also brought the Roman alphabet and a love of learning.

Q. What is pasta?

A. Pasta is made of flour and water. (Sometimes butter, oil, or other things are added for flavor.) After it is mixed, it is rolled out into a thin sheet. Then it is made into everything from spaghetti to macaroni to ravioli.

Q. Where did pizza come from?

A. Pizza is found all over Italy. Each part of the country—and sometimes each town or city—has its own special kind. In some places, there are no tomatoes. In others, a different kind of cheese may be used. It's no wonder that people in Italy love it so much—there are so many different kinds!

Q. Who were the Romans?

A. The Romans ruled Italy—and much of the rest of the world—for almost a thousand years. Their capital was the city of Rome, where many Roman buildings can still be seen. The Roman Empire finally came to an end around 550 A.D. After that, modern Italy began.

Q. What are Russian schools like?

A. Schools in the Soviet Union, which is the real name for what we sometimes call "Russia," are different from ours. Children study many of the same things American children do—math, art, music, language, and other subjects. But they go to school more often. The first four grades in elementary school have classes six days a week. From Monday to Friday, children are in class for about 4½ hours a day. Saturday is a shorter day.

Q. What do Russian children do after school?

A. Russian children enjoy arts and crafts, folk dancing, music, and sports. They also spend time cleaning and fixing up their schools as well as getting ready for plays and holiday pageants.

Q. What kinds of sports do Russian children play?

A. Russian children love sports. There are many special sports clubs for children to enjoy in the Soviet Union. Children start getting serious training in sports by the time they are in nursery school or kindergarten. Soccer is very popular. So are hockey, basketball, skiing, and gymnastics. Chess is also thought of as a sport—and it is very popular.

Q. What is Carnival?

A. Carnival is one of the biggest holidays in Brazil, the largest country in South America. It is one of the greatest parties in the whole world. Thousands of people dress up in costumes. They build giant floats and lead them through the streets. Everyone sings and dances for days.

Q. What kinds of food do people in Brazil eat?

A. People from all over the world settled in Brazil, so they eat all kinds of food. One of the favorites is *churrasco*. It's charcoal-broiled meat, sort of like what you would get at an American barbecue. Brazil's national dish is called *feijoada*. It is made of black beans, beef, and pork.

Q. Who are the *gauchos*?

A. The *gauchos* are the cowboys of Argentina. Argentina has miles and miles of open grasslands. Many years ago, people realized that this land was perfect for raising cattle—and raising beef has become one of the biggest businesses in the country. The *gauchos* have worn special costumes for many years, with balloonlike pants, broad hats, and brightly colored shirts.

HOLIDAYS

HAPPY NEW YEAR

Q. What is a holiday?

A. Our word "holiday" comes from the English term *holy day*. These days were set apart from the usual days of work and play. Sometimes they were for praying or other quiet activities. Other times people had noisy celebrations. For hundreds of years, we have used this word to describe days when we celebrate something.

Q. Why do we celebrate New Year's Day on January 1?

A. People have celebrated the first day of the new year since the beginning of time. But the actual day that people celebrate differs, depending on who you are and where you live. The ancient Romans celebrated the new year on January 1. As time went on, the people ruled by the Romans came to use the Roman calendar—and their new year's day. As a result, much of the world thinks of January 1 as the first day of the year.

Q. How do people celebrate New Year's?

A. In Europe and the United States, New Year's is a very happy holiday. People say good-bye to the old year and wish the new one a warm hello. There are big parties where people wear funny hats and make lots of noise at midnight when the new year begins. In England, people use balloons to help celebrate the new year. They blow up black balloons and kick them out the door at midnight to show that they are getting rid of the bad spirits from the old year.

109

Q. Why do we celebrate the 4th of July?

A. On July 4th, 1776, American leaders signed the Declaration of Independence, which said that the United States was no longer a part of Great Britain. Ever since July 4, 1776, Americans have celebrated Independence Day as their country's birthday—the day on which it became a free country.

Q. What is Memorial Day?

A. Memorial Day is the holiday on which Americans honor all of the soldiers who died fighting in their country's wars. It is the country's way of remembering the thousands of Americans who gave their lives so that our country would be free and safe. People celebrate this day with colorful parades and by putting flowers on soldiers' graves.

Q. How did Memorial Day get started?

A. The very first Memorial Day was actually in the beginning of May. On May 5, 1866, the people of the small town of Waterloo, New York, decided to honor the soliders who died in the Civil War. The idea caught on with other people, and more and more places began to have Memorial Days. The first national observance of Memorial Day was on May 30, 1868. Major General John A. Logan named May 30 as the day to decorate the graves of Northern soliders who died in the Civil War. In order to give people a three-day holiday, Congress changed the celebration to the last Monday in May.

Q. Why do we celebrate George Washington's birthday?

A. We celebrate George Washington's birthday on February 22 every year to show how much we respect and honor this great American. Washington was the very first president of the United States. He was also the leader of the American army in the war for independence. He has been called "the father of his country." In fact, many people believe that without Washington there would have been no United States of America at all.

Q. Why do we celebrate the birthday of Martin Luther King, Jr.?

A. Martin Luther King, Jr. was a great leader in the struggle for equal rights for African-Americans. He believed that the government should treat all people equally, no matter what their color or religion. He also believed that people should live in peace. Because of his beliefs, he used only peaceful means to fight for justice and human rights.

Q. What is Saint Patrick's Day, and why do people wear green on this day?

A. Saint Patrick's Day is held on March 17. It is the feast day of the man who brought the Christian religion to Ireland. People whose families come from Ireland wear green on this day to show their Irish background.

Q. What is Thanksgiving?

A. In the United States, Thanksgiving Day is the holiday on which people give thanks for all of the blessings they have received during the past year. It is a happy holiday when family and friends gather together for feasting and good feelings.

Q. When was the first Thanksgiving?

A. On December 4, 1619, the first settlers from England arrived in Virginia. The laws that the settlers had written for themselves said that the day they got to the New World would be a day of thanks. They fasted, thought about their blessings, and looked forward to a good year. By 1621, the Governor of Massachusetts set aside a special day for giving thanks, too.

Q. Does everyone eat turkey on Thanksgiving Day?

A. Turkey is the most popular meal for Thanksgiving. But many people eat other things. Turkey wasn't even the main part of the meal served at the early Thanksgivings. At those feasts, people of the colony cooked goose, ducks, fish, corn bread, cakes, and vegetables. Their Indian neighbors brought wild turkeys and venison. Everything was cooked on big open fires for several days.

Q. What is Passover?

A. Passover is the Jewish holiday that remembers the people of Israel escaping from slavery in Egypt. This story is told in the Book of Exodus in the Old Testament. Passover usually comes in March or April.

Q. What is a *seder*?

A. A *seder* is a special feast held at Passover time. People read from a book called the *Haggadah*. It tells the story of what happened when Moses led the Israelites out of Egypt.

Q. What special foods are eaten at Passover?

A. There are several special foods served at the Passover *seder*. The most important is *matzo*, which is unleavened bread. It reminds Jews of the flat bread that was made during the forty years the Israelites wandered on their way out of Egypt. Bitter herbs, hard-boiled egg, and the bone of a lamb are also placed on the Passover *seder* table.

Q. When did people start decorating Christmas trees?

A. Christians have celebrated the birth of Jesus since the year 336—over 1,600 years ago. But Christmas trees didn't really become popular until the 1800s. Most people believe that the idea for having a Christmas tree started in Germany.

Q. Does Santa Claus come to everyone in the world?

A. Santa Claus brings presents to children in the United States, Canada, and Australia. In Great Britain, presents come from Santa Claus and Father Christmas. In France, they are brought by *Père Noël;* in Germany, by *Weihnachtsmann,* or "Christmas Man." Saint Nicholas brings presents to children in The Netherlands, Austria, Belgium, and parts of Germany.

Q. Are presents always left under a Christmas tree or in a stocking?

A. In Holland and Austria, children fill their shoes with straw and carrots for Saint Nicholas's horse and place them in front of the fireplace. In the morning, the straw and carrots are gone and presents are there in their place. In Spain, children leave food for the camels of the three Wise Men and put their shoes on the windowsill so that they would be filled with presents.

A. The Festival of Lights is the Jewish holiday of *Hanukkah*, which usually falls around Christmas in December. It celebrates an event that took place over 2,000 years ago, when the Jews in Judea drove the Syrians out of the Temple in Jerusalem. When the people removed the Syrians' idols and statues from the Temple, they found only one small container of oil for lighting their holy lamps. To everyone's surprise, that tiny amount of oil kept the lamps burning for eight days. Ever since, Jews have lit candles and given gifts to remember what happened during that time.

Q. Why do people celebrate Easter?

A. Easter is the most important holiday of the Christian year. It celebrates the death and rebirth of Jesus. It is also a spring holiday. People celebrate the rebirth of plants, sunshine, and other living things after the long dark time of winter.

Q. Why do people give out Easter eggs?

A. In many countries, people give out brightly colored eggs as part of their Easter holiday. No one is sure exactly how eggs became part of Easter. It's probably because eggs stand for a new life—just what Easter celebrates.

Q. What is Lent?

A. Lent is a special religious season for Christians. It begins with Ash Wednesday, 40 days before Easter, and ends with Easter Sunday. It is a time of sadness and seriousness.

Q. Why do people "give something up for Lent"?

A. Lent is a time of sacrifice, and many Christians decide to make a sacrifice of their own by doing without something for the 40 days of Lent. Someone might give up eating meat, going to movies, or even watching television to show they are sincerely sorry for their sins.

Q. Are there any other holidays during which people give something up?

A. Yes. One of the most famous of these is the Jewish holiday of *Yom Kippur*. On *Yom Kippur*, religious Jews *fast*—they do not eat for the entire day. They do this to think about their sins and to ask forgiveness from God. *Yom Kippur* usually comes in September or October.

Q. What is Columbus Day, and how do we celebrate it?

A. Christopher Columbus was a brilliant sailor and sea captain. He is usually thought of as the person who "discovered" America. In August 1492, Columbus and his three ships—the *Niña,* the *Pinta,* and the *Santa Maria*—sailed from Spain. They went westward, hoping to reach China and Japan. Instead, however, they landed on the island of San Salvador in the Bahamas. Columbus's "discovery" brought Europeans to America and changed history. For many years, the date Columbus landed in the New World, October 12th, was set aside as a holiday. We now celebrate Columbus Day on the second Monday in October.

Q. What is Veterans Day?

A. Veterans Day is a holiday that honors American soldiers. We celebrate Veterans Day in many of the same ways we observe Memorial Day, with parades, speeches, and ceremonies at soldiers' graves.

Q. What is Labor Day?

A. Labor Day is a holiday that celebrates all the men and women who work hard for a living. That means people like your family, your teachers, the people who run the stores where you shop, and so on. Labor Day is celebrated on the first Monday in September.

Q. How did Valentine's Day start?

A. Valentine's Day got started in an unusual way. Long ago, in England, people believed that birds chose their mates on February 14, just before the time when the birds laid their eggs. As a result, people began "choosing their mates" on the same day, sending special greetings to the person they loved most. Soon they were sending greetings to everyone else they loved, too.

Q. Who started sending Valentine's Day cards?

A. The first Valentine's Day cards were made by a woman in England named Kate Greenaway. About 100 years ago, she began drawing cards with happy children, pretty gardens, and anything else that meant "Be my valentine."

Q. Do people around the world celebrate Valentine's Day the same way?

A. In the United States, people usually celebrate Valentine's Day by sending cards or flowers to the ones they love. In England, children sing special Valentine's songs and get gifts of candy, fruit, and money. In Denmark, people send white flowers to each other on Valentine's Day. They call these flowers "snowdrops."

119

Q. Why do children go trick-or-treating on Halloween?

A. Trick-or-treating (asking for gifts of candy or money) is the activity most children remember about Halloween. The idea is that children ask for a "treat." Friends and neighbors give out the treats in order to keep the children from playing a nasty "trick" on them.

Q. What do jack-o'-lanterns have to do with Halloween?

A. It wouldn't be Halloween without a jack-o'-lantern. You take a pumpkin and scoop out the inside. Then you cut a face into it. When you're done, you put a candle inside. This lights up the whole face. In England and Ireland, people make their jack-o'-lanterns out of beets, potatoes, or even turnips. But no one is really sure exactly why people started making jack-o'-lanterns on this day.

Q. How did Halloween start?

A. Years ago, people really did believe that Halloween had something to do with spirits. Even before the time of the Romans, people in Britain, Ireland, and northern France had a special holiday on November 1 each year. On the night before that holiday, they honored the ruler of the underworld with bonfires and costumes. As time went on, this holiday became our modern Halloween.

FAMOUS
PEOPLE

Q. Who was the first president of the United States?

A. Our first president, George Washington, was one of the most famous presidents we ever had. Washington was so popular that no one ever really thought of having anyone else be our first president. He's the person you see on the one dollar bill and on a quarter.

Q. Who was Thomas Jefferson?

A. Like George Washington, Jefferson was one of the founders of the United States. In 1776, he wrote The Declaration of Independence. He was a brilliant leader, who was also a great thinker. He started the University of Virginia, designed and built many public buildings, and was a scientist, too. Jefferson was the first president to work and live in Washington, D.C.

Q. What did Betsy Ross do?

A. According to many stories, Betsy Ross made the very first American flag. During the 1770s, she lived in Philadelphia, where she was a seamstress. According to her relatives, a group of Americans led by George Washington came to visit Betsy Ross's sewing shop in 1776. They asked her to make a flag from a rough picture they had drawn. No actual proof of all this has ever been found. We do know that Betsy Ross was the flag maker for the Pennsylvania Navy.

FRANKLIN DELANO ROOSEVELT

RONALD REAGAN

Q. Who was Theodore Roosevelt?

A. Theodore Roosevelt became president in 1901 when he was 43 years old. Roosevelt had been a crime-fighter and a hero of the Spanish-American war. He also helped create the Panama Canal. As a very popular president, he was called "Teddy," which gave rise to the name "teddy bear."

Q. Was there another president named Roosevelt?

A. Yes, Theodore's cousin, Franklin Delano Roosevelt—known as FDR—was also president. He became president in 1933, and he was the only person to ever be president for more than 8 years. FDR was president for 12 years.

Q. Why was John F. Kennedy so famous?

A. John F. Kennedy was the 35th president. He was only 43 years old when he became president in 1960. People all over were excited by his youth, his ideas, and his way of life. He was shot and killed in November 1963.

Q. Why is Ronald Reagan famous?

A. Ronald Reagan was the 40th president. He was also the governor of California and a movie star. Reagan was elected president in 1980 and served for 8 years. He was the oldest person ever to be elected president.

Q. What did Adolf Hitler do during World War II?

A. Adolf Hitler was the leader of the Nazi party that came to power in Germany in 1933. Because of his desire to dominate Europe, he plunged the world into World War II. He led the persecution of millions of people, including Jews, gypsies, and anyone else Hitler thought to be "inferior." Tens of millions of people died because of him.

Q. Who was Winston Churchill?

A. Winston Churchill was the leader of Great Britain during World War II. He helped give his people the will to fight against the Nazis—even though German planes were dropping bombs on them every night. He was again elected Prime Minister after the war, at the age of 77.

Q. What did Mikhail Gorbachev do to make him so famous?

A. Mikhail Gorbachev is President of the Soviet Union and the leader of the Communist Party. He is a very powerful man. In the last few years, he has helped change the face of the world. Gorbachev is giving the people of the Soviet Union and other countries in Eastern Europe more freedom than they have had for years.

Q. Who was Anwar el-Sadat?

A. This Egyptian president who served in the 1970s was famous for creating peace between Egypt and Israel, two countries that had been at war, off and on, for almost 20 years. Sadat was murdered in 1981 by people who were against his peace plans.

Q. Why was Golda Meir famous?

A. Golda Meir was the first woman to be Prime Minister of Israel. Born in the United States, she was a school teacher in Milwaukee, Wisconsin, before moving to Israel. In Israel, she helped create the new country and became its leader.

Q. Is there another woman Prime Minister?

A. Yes, Margaret Thatcher has served as the leader of Great Britain since 1979. She was the first woman to ever hold that office. Since her election, she has led her country in both peace and war. Margaret Thatcher did not start out in politics, though. She studied chemistry at the university and, when she graduated, first went to work as a chemist. She also studied law and became a tax attorney in 1953.

Q. Is the pope always a famous person?

A. Not all popes have been well known. Some led very quiet lives. Pope John Paul II, however, is recognized all over the world. Born in Poland in 1920, he is one of the most popular popes in history.

Q. What did Lech Walesa do for Poland?

A. Lech Walesa is one of the leaders of modern Poland. During the 1970s, he led a group called *Solidarity* that fought for the rights of workers in Polish factories and shipyards. His success helped all of the people in Poland. In 1983, he won the Nobel Peace Prize—one of the greatest honors anyone can receive.

Q. Who is Mother Teresa?

A. Mother Teresa won the Nobel Peace Prize in 1979. She is a Roman Catholic nun, who has spent her life trying to help the world's poor and hungry. She was born in Yugoslavia in 1910 and went to India in 1930. By 1948, she was working by herself among the poor in Calcutta, one of India's largest and poorest cities. Soon she had a whole group of nuns, called the Missionaries of Charity, working with her.

Q. Who was Mahatma Gandhi?

A. Mohandas Gandhi was one of the founders of the free nation of India. For dozens of years, he fought to free his country from the rule of Great Britain. Unlike many other freedom fighters, Gandhi did not believe in the violence of war. Instead, he believed that people could gain freedom without hatred and violence. His love of peace won him the name *Mahatma,* meaning "Great Soul," among the people of India. Unfortunately, not everyone in India agreed with his beliefs. He was murdered in 1948.

Q. Who was Martin Luther King, Jr.?

A. Born in 1929, Martin Luther King, Jr. was one of the most important leaders of the Civil Rights Movements in the United States. For years, he worked tirelessly to get equal rights for all Americans. He used peaceful demonstrations to gain people their freedom and rights. King was murdered in 1968.

Q. Who is Nelson Mandela?

A. Nelson Mandela is one of the most famous leaders among the people of South Africa. During the 1960s, he was put in jail for his efforts to free black Africans from *apartheid,* a system that keeps blacks and whites completely separate. He spent 27 years in prison before finally being freed in 1990.

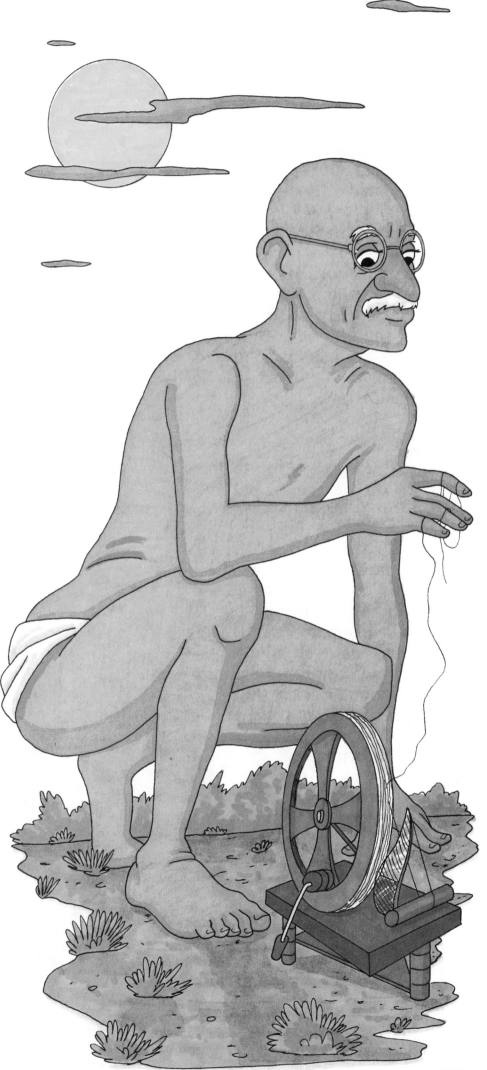

129

Q. Who was William Shakespeare?

A. Shakespeare was probably the greatest—and most famous—writer who ever lived. He lived almost 400 years ago in England. But his plays (stories acted out on stage) are still enjoyed today. Shakespeare wrote romantic stories about love, such as *Romeo and Juliet.* He also wrote plays about the history of England. *Hamlet, Julius Caesar,* and *Macbeth* are three of his most famous tragedies (or sad plays) that are performed often.

Q. Who wrote *A Christmas Carol?*

A. Charles Dickens wrote this famous book. Do you know the story? It's about a mean, stingy man named Scrooge and a sick little boy named Tiny Tim. There have been many movies made from this book. Dickens wrote many books about children growing up in England during the 1800s. *David Copperfield* and *Oliver Twist* are among people's favorites.

Q. Who wrote *Alice in Wonderland?*

A. That story was written by an Englishman named Lewis Carroll in the 1800s. *Alice in Wonderland* is about a little girl who enters a strange underground world of make-believe. Among the unusual characters she meets are Mad Hatter, Cheshire Cat, and Mock Turtle.

130

Q. Who writes plays today?

A. One of the most famous playwrights today is Andrew Lloyd Webber. He wrote *Cats, Starlight Express, Phantom of the Opera,* and *Jesus Christ, Superstar.* As you might guess, because each of these plays has singing and dancing in it, he also writes music.

Q. What songs did Andrew Lloyd Webber write?

A. You have probably heard many of the songs written by this famous British composer. "I Don't Know How To Love Him" (*Jesus Christ, Superstar*), "Don't Cry for Me, Argentina" (*Evita*), and "Memories" (*Cats*) were all written by Andrew Lloyd Webber.

Q. Who wrote *Wizard of Oz*?

A. *Wizard of Oz* was written by Frank L. Baum—a man who used to tell stories to his children and their friends. One day, he decided to write down one of his stories—*The Wonderful Wizard of Oz.* It's all about the adventures of Dorothy, a girl from Kansas, who is picked up by a tornado and carried to a magical land called Oz. Baum wrote many other books about this strange land. When *The Wonderful Wizard of Oz* was made into a movie in 1939, its name was changed to *Wizard of Oz.*

Q. Who were the Marx Brothers?

A. The Marx Brothers were four of the funniest and craziest comedians in history. Their names were funny, too—Groucho, Chico, Harpo, and Zeppo. Groucho was the one with a black moustache, a cigar, and a funny walk. Chico spoke in a funny accent and played the piano. Harpo played the harp—and never said a word. And Zeppo was the young, good-looking one.

Q. Who was Charlie Chaplin?

A. Chaplin was probably the most famous funny man of all time. He usually played "The Tramp," a quiet fellow who was always getting into trouble. He had a funny little moustache, a derby hat, and clothes that never fit. He always ended up making funny faces and being chased away by mean, nasty people. Millions of people laughed at Charlie and his troubles.

Q. Who was the most famous movie star ever?

A. There have been movie stars for almost 100 years. There were stars like William S. Hart (an early Western star) and Mary Pickford ("America's Sweetheart"). Then came Charlie Chaplin. Today's stars are more famous, since movies reach people all over the world. According to most experts, the most famous "star" of all time isn't even a person—it's Mickey Mouse®.

134

Q. Who was Walt Disney?

A. Disney was one of the most famous moviemakers. His specialty was cartoons. In 1928, Disney created one of the most famous cartoon creatures—Mickey Mouse®. During the 1930s, Disney made cartoons that he called *Silly Symphonies*. They starred such wonderful cartoon characters as Mickey Mouse®, Donald Duck®, Goofy®, and Pluto®. Disney also made full-length cartoons. One of the first was *Snow White and the Seven Dwarfs*.

Q. Did Walt Disney start Disneyland®?

A. Yes, the large amusement park was opened in 1955 in Anaheim, California. Many of the exhibits, rides, and shows were based on Disney cartoon characters. Later, in 1971, another Disney park—Walt Disney World®—was opened in Orlando, Florida. The first Disney park that opened outside of the United States was in 1983. This was the Tokyo Disneyland® in Tokyo, Japan.

Q. Who is Steven Spielberg?

A. Spielberg is one of today's most famous moviemakers. His movies are the best known and most popular ones around these days. *E.T.*, *Jaws*, the *Indiana Jones* movies, and the *Back to the Future* movies were all made by Steven Spielberg.

135

Q. Who was Babe Ruth?

A. Babe Ruth was one of the most famous baseball players in history. His first professional job was with the Baltimore Orioles in 1913. In 1914, he went to play for the Boston Red Sox. In 1920, he became a New York Yankee. Babe Ruth hit 60 home runs in 1927. His record stood until 1961, when Roger Maris—another Yankee—hit 61. "The Babe," as he was called, also held the record for the most home runs in a career—714. It wasn't until 1974 that Hank Aaron of the Atlanta Braves broke this record.

Q. Why is Joe DiMaggio famous?

A. Many people think that Joe DiMaggio was the greatest baseball player ever. In 1941, DiMaggio got hits in 56 straight games, which is a record that has never been broken.

Q. Who was Muhammad Ali?

A. Many people think Ali was the greatest boxer who ever lived. He was the heavyweight champion in the 1960s and in the 1970s. He was also an idol for millions of Americans because he spoke out for causes he believed in at the risk of his career.

Q. What sport did Chris Evert Lloyd play?

A. Chris Evert Lloyd is a famous woman tennis player. She turned professional in 1972 at a young age and began winning tournaments almost at once. Over the years, she won just about every major prize in the sport.

BABE RUTH

136

Q. What is the _Mona Lisa_?

A. _Mona Lisa_ is the name of a famous 16th century painting by the famous Leonardo da Vinci. It is the portrait of the wife of a Florentine official. _Mona Lisa's_ smile is famous all over the world. This painting is now at the Louvre, a famous art museum, in Paris, France.

Q. What did Picasso do?

A. Pablo Picasso was a Spanish painter who is probably the most famous artist of the 20th century. His paintings are in museums all over the world.

Q. Who were other famous artists?

A. Many people believe that Leonardo da Vinci, Van Gogh, Rembrandt, and Michelangelo were the most famous artists who ever lived. For many years now, Salvador Dali has been very famous. This Spanish artist worked on everything from oil paintings to plates and dishes. His name and face are recognized everywhere.

Q. Who invented the automobile?

A. The first car to be driven by an engine was built back in 1769 by a Frenchman named Nicholas Cugnot. That machine only traveled at 3 miles an hour and its engine used steam for power. The first gasoline engine car came in 1887. It was invented by Gottlieb Daimler. His name is still around. It's part of the Daimler-Benz company, the people who make Mercedes-Benz cars.

Q. Who were the first people to fly in an airplane?

A. Wilbur and Orville Wright made the first flight in a real aircraft. On December 17, 1903, they flew their plane, *The Flyer,* at Kitty Hawk, North Carolina. The plane went 120 feet in just 12 seconds. Their next flight was even better. It was 852 feet, and the plane stayed in the air for almost a minute.

Q. What did John Glenn do to make him famous?

A. John Glenn was the first American to fly in space. Glenn made his flight in *Friendship* 7 on February 20, 1962. His spacecraft went outside of the earth's atmosphere and went into orbit. After circling the earth three times, he returned to the earth. After he quit being an astronaut, Glenn became a senator for Ohio.

Q. Who was the first person to walk on the moon?

A. The first person to actually set foot on the moon was American astronaut Neil Armstrong. His famous words when he landed in 1969 were: "That's one small step for a man, and a giant leap for mankind."

Q. What did Ben Franklin invent?

A. Benjamin Franklin proved that lightning was really electricity. He also invented the lightning rod. He invented *bifocal* glasses to help people see what's far away and close at the same time. One of his most famous inventions was the Franklin Stove. He helped set up a working post office, the first library in this country, and even started Philadelphia's first fire department.

Q. What inventions was Thomas Alva Edison famous for?

A. Electric light was invented by Thomas Alva Edison. Edison also invented the phonograph. He helped make many other people's inventions work better as well. Among these were the telephone, the typewriter, the motion picture, and many different kinds of electric machines.

Q. Who was Albert Einstein?

A. Einstein was a scientist of the 20th century. His ideas helped other scientists make the first atom bomb. Einstein's famous "Theory of Relativity" came to him when he was 26 years old.

C A P O N E

Q. Who was Jesse James?

A. Jesse James was one of the most famous "outlaws" in American history. Since his death, he has become a legend. Dozens of stories and songs have been written and many movies have been made about him.

Q. What did Billy the Kid do to become famous?

A. Born in Brooklyn, New York, as Henry McCarty, Billy the Kid was one of the most wanted criminals in the West. He lived a life of stealing. Years later, after killing a man, he used the name William Bonney. The first time he was caught, he escaped. Billy the Kid was finally shot on July 17, 1880.

Q. Who were Bonnie and Clyde?

A. Bonnie Parker and Clyde Barrow were an American robbery team in the early 20th century. They became famous through their exciting encounters with the police and the many stories that were written about them in newspapers.

Q. Who was Al Capone?

A. Al Capone was probably the most famous gangster of all time. His gang caused trouble all over Chicago during the 1920s. After many years, the government put him in jail. He was released in 1939 due to illness. Capone died in his Florida estate in 1947.

Q. What is music?

A. Music is the art of organizing sounds, called *tones*, into a specific pattern. A composer—the person who writes music (or puts tones in a pattern)—determines whether they should be loud or soft; how fast they should be at any moment (called *tempo*); and whether the tones should fall, rise, or move straight ahead (called *rhythm*). Often, a composer stresses certain tones. This is called *beat*. When tones are well organized, they can express feelings that words alone could not.

Q. When did music start?

A. Early cave people began singing and making music about 12,000 years ago. Their first musical instruments were made of hollow animal bones. Cave people used music to warn their friends about enemies or nasty animals. They would also sing or play instruments when a baby was born, when someone got married, or even when a hunter brought home something especially good to eat. As time went on, they sang and played music more often and developed different kinds of music.

Q. How can a person's voice make music?

A. It isn't hard to understand how music works. Have you ever hummed a song? If you have, you've made music. Here's how it happens: Close your mouth and hum. Do you hear the musical sounds you are making? You make music through your vocal chords in your throat. When air comes up from your lungs, your vocal chords shake (or *vibrate*).

Q. Why is music important?

A. Most people think music makes them feel good. It can even help people get in a good mood when they're feeling sad. People through the ages used music to help them relax, to celebrate special occasions, and to express feelings and ideas.

Q. What are the different types of musical instruments?

A. One kind is the string instruments—violins, guitars, cellos, and others. Then there are wind instruments like trumpets, saxophones, clarinets, and flutes. Percussion instruments include drums and sound makers like tambourines. Then there are keyboards—pianos and organs. Finally, there's a whole new kind of instrument—electronic ones like electric guitars and synthesizers. They work because of electricity.

Q. How does a wind instrument work?

A. Have you ever seen and heard a nasty storm? Remember how the wind came whistling through the windows? That's how a wind instrument works. Someone blows onto a reed or across a tube and sounds come out. You've probably done this by blowing across the top of an open soda bottle.

Q. How does a string instrument work?

A. String instruments work when someone touches the strings to make them move back and forth, or *vibrate*. To play a violin you need a bow. As you pull the bow back and forth across the strings, sound comes out. Guitars are string instruments, too. Music comes from them when you strum or pull on the strings.

Q. Who invented the violin?

A. Actually, no one person invented the violin. It just developed over hundreds of years. The most famous violin maker was an Italian named Antonio Stradivari. Violins that he made 250 years ago are worth hundreds of thousands of dollars today.

Q. Do record players make music?

A. Most of the music we listen to comes to us through radios, or record, tape, and disc players. However, none of these is an instrument and none of them actually makes music. These players simply play back music that has been recorded somewhere else.

Q. What are percussion instruments?

A. Percussion instruments are very noisy. You make music on them by hitting them with a stick (the way you do with a drum) or by shaking them (the way you do with a tambourine).

Q. How does a keyboard instrument work?

A. A piano is one of the many different kinds of keyboard instruments. How does it work? First, the piano player touches the black-and-white keys on the instrument. These keys then hit small hammers. The hammers then strike the strings that stretch from one end of the piano to the other. The strings make different sounds because each one is a different length. Other keyboard instruments are the organ, clavichord, and harpsichord.

Q. How do electronic instruments work?

A. Electronic instruments make special sounds, although an electric guitar or an electronic piano won't do much of anything without electricity. Once electric power is flowing, the controls on an instrument make all the different sounds that you hear. On an electric guitar, for example, these controls can make the sound high- or low-pitched. Or, they can even make the instrument groan or go "waaahh waaahh" each time the player plucks one of the strings.

Q. What is rock music?

A. Rock music started out in the 1950s as a combination of country and western and rhythm and blues. "Rock" music greats of the 1950s and 1960s were Elvis Presley and The Beatles. The New Kids on the Block, Paul McCartney, and Michael Jackson all play rock music.

Q. Who was Elvis Presley?

A. Elvis was one of the most important rock 'n' roll stars who ever lived. When Elvis first appeared, his handsome face, wonderful voice, and wild way of moving made him a star overnight, although some people were shocked. In fact, when he appeared on television for the first few times, the people in charge of the TV networks only allowed him to be seen from the waist up so the audience couldn't see his wild dancing.

Q. Were The Beatles as famous as Elvis?

A. Yes. The Beatles were four young men from England who wrote and sang some of the best-known songs of the 1960s. "I Wanna Hold Your Hand," "Help," "Yesterday"—they seemed to have one hit after another. By the time the group broke up in the early 1970s, they had sold more records than anyone in history.

Q. What is jazz?

A. No one really knows how to talk about jazz. It can be fast, slow, loud, soft, or it can be a song we can all sing along with. It can also be something with almost no melody at all. Jazz can be played by one person, or by a huge band of fifty or sixty. What really makes jazz different is how it's played. The musicians don't play the music the same way every time. Jazz musicians play the music the way their feelings take them.

Q. What is improvisation?

A. Improvisation is doing something without any real rules. Those are made up as you go along. Jazz musicians may play a fast song slow or a slow song fast. They might even change the tune a bit. They just play a song the way they feel like playing it. Sometimes the result is quite good.

Q. Where did jazz come from?

A. African-Americans were the first people to play jazz more than 100 years ago. Jazz, rock 'n' roll, blue grass, and country and western are the only kinds of music that actually began here in the United States. All other types of music were started in other countries.

Q. What is classical music?

A. Classical music is a type of serious music that was composed mostly in the late 18th and early 19th centuries. Very often, classical music expressed ideas rather than feelings. Beethoven, Mozart, and Haydn were all famous classical music composers. During this time, the piano became a very popular musical instrument. People also enjoy dancing to classical music in the form of ballet.

Q. What is a symphony orchestra?

A. A symphony orchestra is a group of about 100 musicians that plays classical music. There are four main kinds of instruments. The string section consists of the violin, viola, cello, double bass, and harp. The wind instruments are the flute, oboe, clarinet, and bassoon. The brass family is the trumpet, French horn, trombone, and tuba. The percussion instruments are the timpani (or kettledrum), gong, cymbals, triangle, tambourine, and others.

Q. What does an orchestra's conductor do?

A. The conductor is the orchestra's leader. In a way, he or she plays the orchestra like a musical instrument with his or her arms and baton. The conductor tells the musicians when to play, when to stop, and how the music should sound. He or she might want it fast or slow, loud or soft.

Q. What is an opera?

A. An opera is like a play set to music, with all of the characters singing instead of talking. It has just about every form of entertainment imaginable. The stories are usually grand and have lots of exciting action. There are also fancy costumes, stage sets, and lots of special effects.

Q. Who invented opera?

A. A man named Jacopo Peri produced the very first opera back in 1600. It was called *Euridice.* Since then, thousands of operas have been written—and millions and millions of people have gone to see them.

Q. What is folk music?

A. Folk music is the music that ordinary people sing. Songs like "Old McDonald" and "Oh, Susannah" are old folk songs. But in the 1960s, folk music became very popular. Dozens of young singers found and sang tunes that had been around for hundreds of years. Other singers began to write "folk songs." These were songs about what was wrong with our world—prejudice, pollution, and even war.

Q. What is country and western music?

A. Just a few years ago, country and western music was heard only in the South and West of the United States where it was first sung. Today, it's popular just about everywhere. Country music imitates the folk and cowboy styles of music. It almost always tells a story—whether it be sad or happy. Even to this day, most country and western musicians wear cowboy clothes.

Q. Who are some famous country singers?

A. There are many of them—Willie Nelson, Loretta Lynn, and Glen Campbell. Some sing "Nashville"-type songs. Others, like Emmylou Harris, sing songs that are simpler, more like what people might have sung a hundred years ago. Performers like Waylon Jennings even sing music that's so different it's known as "outlaw" music.

Q. What is the Grand Ole Opry?

A. The Grand Ole Opry, a nickname for "Grand Old Opera," began as a radio show in 1925 with the best in country music. People all over the country listened to it. Today, it has grown into a whole entertainment park called "Opryland." It's just outside Nashville, Tennessee.

Q. What is the music of Asia like?

A. Asian music is very different from the music played in Europe and America. First of all, the instruments are quite different. Also, Asian music uses a different scale. *Scale* is the set of sounds that are used in music. In western music, there are 8 notes (and 12 steps) in the scale. You may have heard of these notes—do, re, mi, fa, so, la, ti, and do. Chinese music, however, uses only 5 notes in its scale.

Q. How did Chinese music start?

A. Chinese music began thousands of years ago when Chinese music makers were invited to play before the emperor. Since operas were special favorites of the emperor, they were often performed. Opera is still very popular in China.

Q. What kinds of instruments are used in Chinese music?

A. Chinese musicians use many different instruments. Among them are bells, drums, gongs, and flutes. The favorite instruments, however, are the *ch'in* and the *p'i-p'a.* These are like guitars. In fact, some Chinese musicians today play rock 'n' roll on these instruments.

Q. Is Japanese music like Chinese music?

A. Not really. The people of Japan first learned about music from the Chinese. Over time, however, they changed it into something completely their own.

Q. What is Japanese music like?

A. Japanese music uses instruments much like guitars. These are called *samisen* and *koto*. It also uses a flute called *shakuhachi* that is made of bamboo. In Japan, music is usually played and sung without harmony. *Harmony* is the "other voices" besides the main melody that you hear in a song.

Q. What kinds of instruments are used in Indian music?

A. Indian music has become popular all over the world. The most famous Indian instrument is a kind of long-necked guitar called *sitar.* When people play in public, the *sitar* is usually joined by a drum or *tambour,* which is another stringed instrument. Indian music was first played to please kings (called *maharajas*) and princes.

Q. What is African music like?

A. African music has been around for thousands of years, and it is quite varied. Drums, bells, flutes, and even clapping hands are all used to make music. Music is an important part of the lives of people in Africa. It is used in their religion, in special occasions for families, and even to help people work and play.

Q. What are African drums like?

A. African drums come in all shapes and sizes. Some are made of animal skins. The drummer plays them by tapping on the tight skin with his or her fingers. Others are made from hollow logs. Drummers tap on these with a stick.

Q. How did native American Indians make music?

A. The people who lived in America before Columbus made music for thousands of years. In fact, music has always been a big part of their lives. When people went hunting, for example, they sang special songs. There were also songs that were supposed to help people get well or to bring rain. People usually played drums and rattles as they sang.

TELEVISION

Q. What was the first real American program?

A. The first real show that people saw on TV was in 1939. During the World's Fair in New York City, countries from all over the world put on shows and exhibits. The National Broadcasting Company—NBC as it is still called today—sent out TV pictures of President Franklin D. Roosevelt making a speech at the Fair. Only about 1,000 people got to see the pictures, though. There weren't many TV sets around.

Q. What did early TV sets look like?

A. Early TVs looked very different from the ones we have now. The screens were tiny. Some were only a few inches across. But the sets were big and heavy. There were few to buy and they were very expensive.

Q. Why are there commercials on TV?

A. In the United States, most TV shows get on the air because the station sells time to companies. Companies use this time, called *commercials*, to tell people about their products to tempt them to buy. The money that comes in from these companies is used to pay for the shows that go on the air.

Q. Does everyone in the country watch the same TV stations?

A. There are thousands of TV stations around the country. Each one sends out programs to an area less than 100 miles away from it. We all watch the local station in our area. Many of these local stations belong to large groups called *networks*. There are three big TV networks in the United States. They are the American Broadcasting Company (ABC), the Columbia Broadcasting System (CBS), and the National Broadcasting Company (NBC). Each one sends out shows to the local stations in its network.

Q. Why do people say they are "shooting" a movie or TV program?

A. When camera operators point cameras and start to take pictures, they are "shooting." The word probably comes from the fact that you aim a camera just like you aim a gun.

Q. What is a "live" show?

A. Most shows are shown on film or videotape. Other shows are put on the air while they are happening. News shows and sports shows are often seen this way.

Q. Why do you hear background laughter during a comedy show?

A. In the early days of television, TV people began putting laughter into the shows. They paid audiences to come and watch shows as they were made—and to laugh. Sometimes, they just added the sound of laughter to film or videotape. Today, many actors like to work on a stage with people in the audience. When a show recorded in front of an audience is shown on TV, you can hear the sounds of the audience all during the show.

Q. What is prime time?

A. In the evening, when people are ready to relax for a while, millions of television sets click on all over the country. The most popular time to watch TV is between 8 o'clock and 11 o'clock at night, or between 7 o'clock and 10 o'clock, depending on where you live. This is called *prime time*.

Q. What is a rerun?

A. A rerun is a show that is being shown—or "run"—again. It is also called a "repeat." A show that is a rerun is often marked with the letter *R* in your TV schedule.

Q. What kind of puppets are the Muppets?

A. There are, as you know, many different Muppets, and they work in different ways. Some are hand puppets. Others work with sticks that make the arms move up, down, and around. Others work with strings. Big Bird™ actually has a person inside, walking, talking, and moving around. How many people do you think are inside Barkley™ or Snuffy™?

Q. How long has *Sesame Street™* been on television?

A. *Sesame Street™* has been on TV since the late 1960s. One of your parents might have watched it when he or she was little. Characters like Kermit the Frog™, Oscar the Grouch™, Cookie Monster™, Bert™ and Ernie™, the Count™, Grover™, and Big Bird™ are loved by millions of kids. *Sesame Street™* has been translated into other languages, so that children all over the world can get to know the people and Muppets of the show.

Q. Is there really a Mr. Rogers' neighborhood?

A. Fred Rogers' show comes to you from Pittsburgh, Pennsylvania, and many of his guests live around that city. But, as you probably know, *Mr. Rogers'® Neighborhood* is really make-believe. The houses, cars, and stores you see on each show are models.

Q. How are cartoons made?

A. Suppose you wanted to make a cartoon of someone waving his or her arm. You'd start with a picture of that person with an arm by his or her side. Your next picture would be of the same person, but his or her arm would be moved up just a little bit. In the next picture, the arm would be moved up a little bit more. You would continue drawing pictures until the person's arm was all the way up and waving. It takes hundreds of pictures to do this, but when you stack the pictures in order and flip through them, the picture looks like it is moving.

Q. Have there always been cartoons on TV?

A. Cartoons have been on TV almost since the beginning. Bugs Bunny®, Elmer Fudd®, Daffy Duck®, Mickey Mouse®, Road Runner®, and dozens of other cartoon favorites have been dashing around on TV screens for years.

Q. Was Saturday morning always cartoon time?

A. The people who make TV shows know that children aren't in school on Saturday morning. Almost from the beginning of TV, children's shows were on the air on Saturday mornings. Some of these shows have live people, games, and other kinds of fun. Most of them, however, are cartoons.

A. The news is the story of what is happening—in your home town, around the country, and around the world. TV news is like a newspaper that moves and talks. It shows you the important stories about current events—what governments and leaders are doing as well as sports scores and human interest stories.

Q. How do news announcers know what's going on in the world?

A. It takes many people to let your TV news announcers know what is happening around the world. TV networks have reporters and camera operators in almost every large city in the world. They also send reporters on *assignment* to go to certain places because something important is happening there. Your local TV station also has its own reporters. These announcers, writers, and camera operators cover the important events happening in your area. Reporters ask questions, take pictures, go on camera to explain what is happening, and then rush off to cover the next story.

Q. Who decides what news goes on the air?

A. Most TV news shows have a managing editor who looks over the different news stories and decides which ones to show on TV. Writers work on these stories, trying to explain events clearly and quickly.

Q. What is a sports special?

A. Some sports events, such as the Super Bowl, the World Series, the Olympics, and the Indianapolis 500 are very interesting to people. TV networks send special crews to go to these events and bring them to you on TV.

Q. What is a soap opera?

A. Daytime story dramas called *soap operas* tell stories filled with the troubles and difficulties faced by a group of people. There is little action, but there is a lot of romance. Soap operas got their name in a strange way. Years ago, in the days of radio, soap operas were popular with women who stayed home and took care of their families. So many of the shows were put on by soap and cleaning product companies that everyone soon started calling these dramas "soaps."

Q. What is a western?

A. Westerns are shows about cowhands and other people from the days of the old Wild West. They have been on TV from the beginning. In fact, some of the most popular shows of all time—such as *Bonanza* and *Gunsmoke* were westerns.

GAMES & TOYS

Q. How long have children been playing with toys?

A. No one knows for sure exactly when toys were first made or what the first toys were like. Most likely, cave people made rattles or other toys out of animal bones or rock. By the time of the ancient Egyptians 5,000 years ago, children had all kinds of toys. There were balls, pulling toys, and even toy animals. Children in ancient Greece and Rome even had toy boats and hoops. In fact, toys really didn't change all that much until the 1900s, when electric toys were first made.

Q. How do tops stay up?

A. When tops spin, they make a special kind of force that keeps them standing up. It doesn't matter whether the top works with a string, a spring, or even an electric motor. Once it starts turning around and around, it will keep going for a long time until it begins to slow down.

Q. Do all children play with tops?

A. Tops are found just about everywhere. Children in China and Japan have been playing with them for thousands of years. In Europe and America, string tops were used for ages. Native American children made tops out of hollowed-out nuts. Eskimo children made their tops out of the ivory of a walrus tusk.

Q. Do all children like to play with dolls?

A. Most children seem to love playing with small toys that look like human beings. Some like dolls that are all dressed up in fancy clothes. Others like action figures such as G.I. Joe®. It was not until the 1700s that dolls became popular toys for children.

Q. How are dolls made today?

A. Today, dolls are made of plastic and other man-made materials. First, an artist draws a picture. Then, metal *molds*—shape makers like the ones you use for making cookies or cupcakes—are made from the picture. When plastic is poured into these molds, it forms the shape of a doll. Then, people paint the "skin" of the doll, add eyes and hair, and sew a doll's clothing.

Q. What are some famous dolls?

A. Certainly the Barbie® doll, Raggedy Ann®, and the Cabbage Patch Kids™ have become very famous. But the most famous doll of all is hardly ever seen in toy stores. It is called the Kewpie® doll. It was created in the early 1900s by an American artist named Rose O'Neill. She made it look like her baby brother. The Kewpie® doll became famous because it was used as a prize in carnivals, games, and all kinds of contests.

Q. Are stuffed animals toys?

A. A toy is anything that people like to play with. Stuffed animals are among the most popular toys. Children like to cuddle with their stuffed animals. They like to use their imaginations and play with them, too.

Q. How did the teddy bear get its name?

A. Believe it or not, the teddy bear was named for a president of the United States—Theodore Roosevelt. Roosevelt was famous as a hunter and lover of the outdoors. During one of his hunting trips, he helped save a baby bear's life. The story became famous all over the country. Since Roosevelt's nickname was "Teddy," toy makers quickly brought out a stuffed bear named for the president—and the famous baby bear. And with that, "teddy bears" began turning up everywhere.

Q. What are the best kinds of roller skates?

A. Roller skates work best if they are part of a boot or shoe. That way, they don't slip around. You can make turns better, too. It used to be very expensive to make skates this way. Now, because of plastics, it is easy and inexpensive to make skates that are fixed to boots.

Q. What are skateboards made of?

A. Skateboards are usually made of fiberglass or wood. They are flat shapes wide enough for a person to stand on. Wheels are attached under the board. These are usually made of a plastic called *urethane*. Plastic wheels turn faster and smoother than metal ones.

Q. How did skateboards get started?

A. Believe it or not, skateboards got started because there weren't any waves in the ocean! In California during the 1950s, people who loved surfing often had to sit around waiting until the waves got big enough for them to use their surfboards. To kill time, they started hooking roller skates to the bottoms of surfboards. Then, they could "surf" along the street and sidewalk. Soon, they found that boards worked better if they were smaller and lighter. By the early 1960s, a new, exciting kind of toy had been invented.

Q. How does a Slinky® work?

A. Slinkys® "walk" because of the way the coils of wire are hooked together—and because of their weight. When the first coils go in one direction, the others follow because they are attached. They speed up and "slink"—the weight of the first coils pulls the rest of the Slinky® along.

173

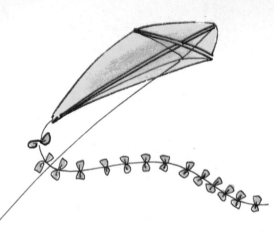

Q. **Who invented kites?**

A. No one knows. What we do know is that the Chinese first used kites almost 5,000 years ago. About 2,200 years ago, they used kites during wars. These kites had bamboo pipes on them, which would make strange noises to frighten the enemy.

Q. **How do kites fly?**

A. Kites fly because of the force of air. When you want to get a kite up into the air, the first thing to do is to get its nose up into the wind. When this happens, there is more force from the air in front than in back. This lifts the kite up into the air.

Q. **Have kites been used for other reasons besides fun?**

A. In the 1840s, people were building a bridge across the Niagara River to connect the United States and Canada. Giant kites were flown up into the air to carry the bridge's cables over the river. Once the cables were on the other side, the workers could use them to hang the bridge over the river.

Q. **What experiment did Benjamin Franklin do with a kite?**

A. Back in the 1700s, Benjamin Franklin flew a kite up into the air during a lightning storm. When the electricity from a bolt of lightning traveled down the kite's string to a key on the ground, Franklin discovered that lightning contained electricity.

Q. Where did Frisbees® come from?

A. Many people say that the Frisbee® was invented by a man named Fred Morrison, from Los Angeles. This round, flat plate has been around for about 25 years.

Q. How do you play jacks?

A. To play jacks, you need six jacks and a small rubber ball. You play by bouncing the ball and scooping up jacks with your hand. You have to catch the ball without dropping the jacks. Sometimes, people try to pick up all of the jacks at once. Other times, they pick up one, two, or even three at a time. Did you know that people have been playing games like jacks ever since the time when people lived in caves? Scientists have found pieces of this game that are thousands and thousands of years old.

Q. When have hula hoops been popular?

A. Hula hoops first became popular almost forty years ago, during the 1950s. People kept the hoop spinning by moving back and forth and around. After a while, hula hoops began to disappear. In the 1980s, they became popular again. Children were once again swiveling around to keep these brightly colored rings of plastic twirling around their bodies.

Q. Do all model trains run on electricity?

A. Many of the most popular kinds of model trains use electricity to pull the cars. But even today you can buy model trains that work on wind-up springs. Some even work on gravity—they get their speed and movement by moving downhill.

Q. Are children the only people who like model trains?

A. Most children love model trains. But there are almost 225,000 adults who belong to model train clubs. They build very fancy systems for their trains, with mountains, trees, rivers, and even towns and cities. In fact, some of the railroad systems they make look so real that you could almost mistake them for places you've seen before.

Q. What kinds of models are there?

A. You can make a model of anything—a plane, a ship, a car, or even a building. Some models are easy to build, with just a dozen or so pieces. Others are very complicated and take thousands of pieces and many hours to build. There are even model cars with real engines that are big enough to ride in. It takes a lot of work—and help from grown-ups—to make them.

Q. Why are some games called board games?

A. In a board game, the players move pieces around on a flat surface called a *board*. A board is usually marked in some way so that players know where and how to move. Board games include Monopoly®, Parcheesi, Clue® and Wheel of Fortune. Board games are very popular and they've been around for a long time. Pictures on the wall in an Egyptian pyramid show Queen Nefertiti playing a board game. She lived 4,500 years ago!

Q. Why do people shout out "Bingo!" when they play that game?

A. People shout "Bingo!" to tell the other players that they have won. To play Bingo, you need a card covered with different numbers. The numbers are printed in rows across the card. One person spins a wheel and picks a number. If a player has that number, he or she covers it with a piece of plastic. When a player covers up a whole row of numbers, he or she shouts "Bingo."

Q. Where did playing cards start?

A. Playing cards probably started in India in the 8th century. At first, cards were used to tell fortunes and they looked very different. There were 78 cards in a deck. The first deck of 52 cards was made in France in the 1500s.

Q. When did children start to play with marbles?

A. Back in the Stone Age, people made marbles out of baked clay. Today, children play marbles just about everywhere in the world. In South America, marbles are called *bolitas*. In China, children kick marbles. In Iran, they use marbles made from baked mud or small stones.

Q. How do you play marbles?

A. To play marbles, you need a "shooter" marble and some "play" marbles. You take your shooter marble and, using your thumb and first finger, "shoot" it at the play marbles. You keep shooting at them until you knock them all out of a circle.

Q. How did laser tag get its name?

A. Laser tag is pretty much like the old-fashioned game of tag—except that you tag the other players by using a blast from a harmless laser gun. The light from the gun sets off a light or sound on the costumes that all players wear. That way everyone knows when someone's been tagged. There's no cheating in this game!

Q. What is an electronic game?

A. Electronic games are really small computers. Running the game is a set of instructions, called a *program*. Most electronic games are connected to a special viewing screen where you can see all of the action. That's why the games are usually called *video games*—they have video screens, just like TVs.

Q. What is Pong®?

A. Pong® was the first real video game to become popular. It came out in the early 1970s and was a big hit with everyone. All you did was hit a ball back and forth across a line in the middle of the TV screen.

Q. What are word games?

A. Word games are played with words and imagination. The most famous word game is probably Twenty Questions. In that game, one player thinks of something that is animal, vegetable, or mineral. The other players ask questions about that object until they can guess what it is.

Q. What is Charades?

A. Charades is a special kind of word game. One player thinks of something to act out. It can be a song, the name of a TV show, or anything. He or she acts it out, without speaking, until his or her team guesses what it is.

Q. Are there games that use pictures?

A. In some games, people have to draw pictures instead of act out the words. You can even make up these games yourself. Just write down sayings, place names, song titles, and other words on slips of paper. Put them in a hat for people to select. Then just divide your friends into teams and play.

Q. What are fantasy games?

A. Did you ever hear of Dungeons and Dragons®? It's one of the most popular fantasy games around. Fantasy games take a great deal of imagination to play. In Dungeons and Dragons®, the players move through deep, dark dungeons, fight fierce monsters, and try to capture wonderful treasures.

Q. How are war games played?

A. There are all kinds of war games. Some like Stratego® and Battleship are played on boards. These games use miniature soldiers, ships, and other weapons. Other war games are played with only your imagination. You must try to outsmart and "outfight" the other player. Sometimes, you do this on a board. Other times, you use a map that shows a real battlefield from history. Some games are even played with a small computer. No matter how they are played, war games can be exciting.

Q. Why do people in different parts of the world dress differently?

A. People live in different climates. Some places are hot and dry. Other places are hot and wet, cold and wet, or cold and dry. People wear different clothes to help them stay warm, dry, or cool. People also live in different cultures. *Culture* is the kinds of houses people live in, their language, their religion, their stories and history, and the ways they have fun. The clothing people wear also shows their culture.

Q. What are different clothes made of?

A. The cloth your clothes are made of might be wool (if it's cold outside), cotton (if it's summertime), nylon, or a combination—like polyester and cotton. *Polyester* is a material people make from chemicals. You can't grow it or find it in nature. Cloth has also been made from softened tree bark. Linen cloth is made from tall, grassy plants called *flax*. Cloth is also made from camel or goat hair or cow leather.

Q. Why do clothing styles change?

A. The clothing industry is a big business. Many people work at designing, making, and selling new clothes. If designers did not constantly change the way clothes looked, people would not buy nearly as many clothes as they do now.

Q. Why do men wear ties?

A. For years, men have worn ties to show they are successful. They choose ties of a certain style, size, and color, depending on what is popular. Of course, some men think ties are a joke. They wear silly ties or ones in the shape of fish.

Q. What is the difference between a shirt, a blouse, and a T-shirt?

A. Mostly men wore shirts when they first appeared in the 1500s. The blouse did not appear until the mid-1800s. Worn mainly by women, blouses had high collars, fitted cuffs, and full sleeves. The T-shirt became popular in this century. It has short sleeves and no collar.

Q. Why do men's shirts button on the right side and women's shirts on the left side?

A. In the 1400s only rich people wore buttons. However, even rich men usually dressed themselves. It was easier for them to button from right to left. Rich women usually had maids to help them dress. Maids also buttoned right to left. But they were facing the shirt, not looking down at it.

Q. How did people fasten their clothes before they used buttons?

A. Buttons have been around for thousands of years. But until about 700 years ago, buttons were not used to fasten clothing together. They were used to decorate clothes. Special buttons made of gold, silver, and jewels were also used as money. Clothes were fastened with pins, strings, and hooks.

Q. What are buttons made of?

A. Most buttons today are made of plastic. You'll also find buttons made of metal, leather, pearl, and shell. In the past, buttons were made of ivory or bone, gold and silver, brass, wood, and ceramics. Rich people had diamond and jade buttons. Buttons have also been made out of nuts and glass. What are your buttons made of?

Q. How does Velcro® work?

A. Velcro® is made of two nylon strips. One strip has tiny hooks, like the hooks on sticky thistle burrs. The other strip has tiny eyes, something like the loops of thread that burrs stick to on people's clothes. When the two strips are pressed together, the hooks lock into the eyes. They can be opened by pulling them apart. The name comes from "vel" in *velvet* and "cro" in *crochet,* the French word for "hook."

Q. When did women start wearing skirts?

A. Actually, at one time both men and women wore robes. Then western (meaning European) men started wearing pants about 2,500 years ago and women's long robes became dresses. When people started making outfits in separate pieces, the skirt was separated from the top of the dress. Then many women began wearing skirts and blouses as well as dresses.

Q. Do men ever wear skirts?

A. In the Western world, some Scottish men wear skirts called *kilts*. These knee-length kilts are made in many different colors of wool plaids. Each plaid stands for a different family. In hot desert countries, some men wear loose flowing robes, which are cooler than pants. In some hot tropical countries, men often wear what look like short skirts to help them stay cooler.

Q. Why do people worry about skirt lengths?

A. The accepted length for skirts has gone from the floor to above mid-thigh and places in between. For some reason, a change in length for women's skirts has become the biggest sign that fashion is going through a big change. Some people say women's skirts go up and down with the rise and fall of the country's wealth. Now, many women refuse to let fashion tell them how long or short to wear their skirts.

Q. What did the first shoes look like?

A. The first shoes were sandals worn by ancient Egyptians. Rich people wore sandals with pointed toes. Sandals were often made of woven plant reeds. People in colder places wore pieces of animal skin around their feet.

Q. When did people start wearing left and right shoes?

A. You know you have a left and a right foot. But long ago, the difference in feet made no difference. Each shoe in a pair was exactly alike. People's shoes were not very comfortable. In the 1800s, the *last* was invented. A last is a foot-shaped block that leather can be fitted over to be made into a shoe. This way, left and right shoes could be made and walking became a more pleasant activity.

Q. Why do people wear different kinds of shoes?

A. People need different shoes for different activities. Boots are for playing in snow and walking in rain. Sneakers are for running and loafers for loafing. Dress shoes dance and work shoes work. Sandals are great for the beach and slippers keep your feet warm at home. But sometimes bare feet are best of all.

Q. Why do people put on special clothes to go swimming?

A. Regular clothes usually become much heavier when they are wet. They also cling to the body. It also takes a long time for regular clothes to dry once they get wet. So people wear specially made, light clothing that is meant to get wet and dries quickly.

Q. Did swimsuits always look like they do now?

A. When people first started to swim for fun and better health in the mid-1800s, they wore bathing suits that looked like street clothes. Women wore a knee-length dress with stockings and canvas shoes. Men wore almost the same thing. These clothes became so heavy when they got wet that they were dangerous. No one could swim in them. In 1915, Carl Jantzen invented an elastic, lightweight sweater material that was comfortable to swim in.

Q. Why do people wear hats?

A. Hats can protect people from rain, sun, cold or from falling objects. They can also show what job a person does. A chef wears a tall white hat. A construction worker wears a hard hat that covers his head. A nurse wears a white, pointed hat. A king and a queen wear crowns to show they are rulers. People also wear hats for fun or to make their outfits stylish.

Q. What styles have been the most uncomfortable for people to wear?

A. Throughout the history of clothing, people have made up some styles to wear that made no sense in terms of comfort. In the Middle Ages, the points on shoes were so long people could hardly walk without tripping. In the 1500s, heels became so high that walking became a problem again. In the 1800s, women suffered from tight corsets and from trying to sit with hoop skirts flying up in their faces.

Q. What do fire fighters wear to protect themselves?

A. Fire fighters have to wear clothing made out of special materials to protect them from heat, flames, and smoke. They wear jackets, pants, and boots made out of material that is flameproof and waterproof. They use gloves and hats that won't burn.

Q. Why did people start wearing nightgowns to bed?

A. In the 1600s, people wore many layers of stiff clothes. At night, they were happy to put on more comfortable, long, loose shirts. These became "nightgowns." People also wore them to bed to keep warm.

Q. How were jeans invented?

A. During the California gold rush in the 1850s, a clothes maker named Levi Strauss saw how quickly miners wore out their pants. He started making sturdier ones out of thick canvas. They sold well. Then Levi found a softer material called *denim.* He dyed it dark blue so that it wouldn't show dirt stains. They became a hit and were called *Levi's*® in honor of their maker.

Q. Why are jeans so strong?

A. The denim cloth jeans are made from is woven very tightly out of very strong thread. At one time, the pockets were made stronger with copper rivets or metal buttons inserted at the end of each pocket seam. Now the pockets are made stronger with metal studs.

Q. What can a handkerchief be used for?

A. People once used handkerchiefs to blow their noses. Now they use throw-away tissues. Cowboys used kerchiefs called *bandannas* for many things. They kept the dust out of noses and mouths, wrapped a cut, held a broken arm, tied a hat on in strong winds, kept the sun off the neck, and strained dirt from water.